"Their Name
is Wicks..."

"Their Name is Wicks..."

ONE FAMILY'S JOURNEY
THROUGH SHAKER HISTORY

Dear Annette,
Peace + Simplicity —
Good Guidelines for life!
Best,

Ann C. Sayers

Book Design by The Troy Book Makers

Printed in the United States of America

The Troy Book Makers • Troy, New York • thetroybookmakers.com

To order additional copies of this title, contact your favorite local bookstore or visit www.tbmbooks.com

ISBN: 978-1-61468-374-2

To my family,
most especially to Peter, my rock.

ACKNOWLEDGEMENTS

When I was growing up, our family used to go by the Ann Lee Nursing Home, near what is now the Albany International Airport, when we happened to be en route to pick up or drop off travelers. I wondered who Ann Lee was-- someone who endowed the facility with its name, no doubt. Little did I--an immigrant child with roots in England, born of a Quaker father and Danish mother-- dream that that this oddball mystic from Manchester would lead me deeply into Shaker history, or that I would one day end up writing a book about this remarkable Christian sect.

My first inspiration came from a touching short memoir, "Shaker Days Remembered," by Martha H. Hulings. Hulings spent five years of her childhood--in the early 1920s--living in the South Family at Watervliet. Martha Hulings inscribed her book to me in 1988; she was by then quite an old woman, with a sweet smile and a warm handshake. Her book is filled with vivid scenes of a very happy childhood spent under the mostly gentle tutelage of the Shakers. Hulings particularly remembered Eldress Anna Case as an extraordinarily kind and capable person.

"Shaker Days Remembered" led me to volunteer at the Shaker Heritage Society, and the rest, as we say, is history. More recently, Ann Clothier (now at the Brookside Museum in Ballston Spa) deserves special thanks for sharing a newspaper piece from January 1853, entitled "A Shaker Marriage." It was this article that first drew my attention to the Wicks, and served as a catalyst for my long research journey into the Shaker world.

I owe profound respect to the memory of Betty Shaver, who was an early and dedicated volunteer for many years at the Shaker Heritage Society. Betty delved deeply into Shaker history, and she compiled binder upon binder of transcribed journals and other data, which now reside at the museum, and which offer visitors and scholars an amazing panoramic view of the Watervliet Shakers. I regret that I never found the time to sit at Betty's feet and absorb some of her amazing knowledge. However I did seek out Chris Kelly, Betty Shaver's daughter, who currently serves as the Schaghticoke Town Historian, and who spent hours on several occasions helping me ferret out Wicks family background, and who guided me to various useful resources. Thank you, Chris.

Special thanks to Starlyn D'Angelo, Patti Williams, Samantha Hall-Saladino and Candace Murray at the Shaker Heritage Society, who have been faithful supporters of my Wicks project, encouraging me, and helping in many respects. Also to the librarians at the New York State Library Special Collections, especially to Vicki Weiss; and to the staff at the Hamilton College Special Collections, New York- Historical Society library and the New York Public Library Special Collections. Thanks are due to members of the Shaker Listserv, who directed me to some hidden nuggets; to Glendyne Wergland, who drew my attention to a wonderful online resource on the Prentiss family. Thanks to Don Papson who led me to the Van Hoosen connection.

I am grateful to Roderick Bradford, the author of a most illuminating book, "D.M. Bennett: the Truth Seeker." Rod encouraged me from long distance, and I owe him credit for generously sharing resources on Derobigne Bennett and Mary Wicks. Thank you to my "first readers," Karen Armstrong, Kathy Zdeb, and Scott Gibbs. They helped wrestle the book into shape, and provided invaluable advice/direction. Family friend Nora Ritchie was kind enough to take a field trip to the Green-Wood Cemetery, where she took wonderful pictures of the Wicks Family plot. Mike Zdeb photographed numerous images from the Shaker Collection in the New York State Library for me: I am grateful for his time (not to mention, his Drop Box expertise).

Very special thanks are due to Jodi Miller, who created the book's eye-catching cover, and who provided invaluable advice over design issues ; and to Nick Alberti at the Troy Book Makers, whose frank and kind support helped greatly, especially in the final stretch.

I owe a debt to Ilyon Woo, whose excellent book "The Great Divorce," drew me deeper into the Shaker world, and to Jill Lepore, whose vivid, creative non-fiction served as inspiration. These writers don't know me, but they allowed me to take a risk when my sources were spare; they helped me to imagine the Wicks as a family, to "labor"(as the Shakers did) and bring these special individuals from the past to life again.

A NOTE ON SHAKER "FAMILIES"

The focus of this book revolves mostly around the first Shaker settlement in America, located in Watervliet--once known as Niskayuna, now the town of Colonie, New York. Today, what was the Church Family village is the home of the Shaker Heritage Society, a small museum dedicated to keeping Shaker history alive and pertinent in our busy modern world.

Shakers lived in large groups of 70 to 100 people. These "Families" operated as cooperatives, and members referred to one another as Sisters and Brethren (Brothers). Men and women lived separately--celibacy was a guiding principle--but they worked side-by-side to keep their community going. The most important matters in each Family--spiritual harmony and family balance--were overseen by an Elder and Eldress. These senior leaders were typically mature and wise individuals who often held their positions for many years. Day-to-day matters in each Family were directed by carefully chosen Brethren and Sisters known as Deacons and Deaconesses. In larger families, sometimes more than one person was needed in such positions, hence "First Deaconess, Second Deaconess." These trusted and capable members faced the huge job of maintaining order among many dozens of people: seeing to it that newcomers found good roommate matches, that seating in the dining room made equitable sense, that every dwelling room was adequately furnished, that the books in the library were shared appropriately, that general supplies were adequately provided, etc. Because of the stress of managing day-to-day life for so many people, Deacons and Deaconesses sometimes "burned out," and took breaks from the job.

The most experienced (senior) Believers generally lived in the CHURCH FAMILY (sometimes organized into two Families called the First Order and the Second Order); this was the site of the Meeting House, where the whole community--all members of all of the families--met for worship on Sunday, the Sabbath Day. As the population expanded, new families were organized, and these were often designated by compass coordinates: hence, when a new family group was formed at Watervliet, it became known as "The South Family." The next family became the "West Family," and finally at Watervliet there was the "North Family." Every Shaker community had what was called "The Gathering Order," where prospective converts stayed during their introductory period, until they signed the Covenant (the religious document which indicated one's devotion) and became Committed Believers. At Watervliet, the main Gathering Order was The South Family. As the years passed and Shaker populations swelled, children were organized into separate units, sometimes called "the Children's Order," or "The Girls Shop" and "The Boys Shop." There was also a place that functioned as an infirmary in every community, often called "The Second House."

What remains of the Church Family site at Watervliet, as well as the famous Shaker Cemetery (where Mother Ann's body is buried), can still be viewed by taking a walking tour of the grounds. The 1848 Meeting House has recently been renovated, and presently houses the offices and museum space for the Shaker Heritage Society. Both the Meeting House and the newly restored (circa 1915) Barn are currently used for various museum and community-based events. However other Shaker buildings at the site have fallen into disrepair. As of this writing, significant structures from the Watervliet West Family property--recently sold to a developer-- can be viewed from the Albany-Shaker Road near the Albany International Airport. Plans are evolving to study and preserve some of this valuable Shaker property.

The various Family Names mentioned in Shaker documents can be confusing. Whenever possible, I have used the simple compass coordinates of Family Names, and I refer to all those in the various Church Orders as simply the "The Church Family." Note that in the journals, the writers often use initials: CF for Church Family, SF for South Family, etc.

Throughout this book I include quotations from Shaker journals, to give the reader a flavor of what daily life was like almost 200 years ago in "Wisdom's Valley," as the Watervliet site was sometimes later known. "WV" was the acronym for this community, and "NL" was the acronym for the New Lebanon/Mount Lebanon community. The New Lebanon Shaker community, near the Massachusetts border, served as the main Ministry, or Bishopric, for all of the Shaker villages in the northeast.

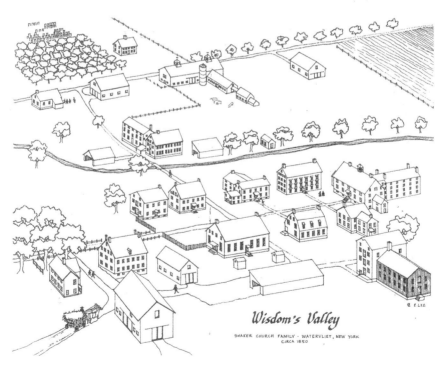

Wisdom's Valley

SHAKER CHURCH FAMILY · WATERVLIET, NEW YORK
CIRCA 1850

Shaker Heritage Society
Courtesy of artist Libby Lee

LIST OF CHARACTERS

[Spelling was inconsistent: Wicks appears as "Wickes," or "Weeks" or even "Wix." Wicks seems the most common version.

The Wicks Family

Job Wicks: born in Rhode Island in 1769 to Thomas and Sarah Wicks, a Quaker couple.

Polly (Prentiss) Wicks: born in Deerfield, Massachusetts, February 2, 1786 (and see below).

Their children (all except the eldest were born in Reading, Steuben County, New York):

Nancy: born in Chenango County, September 14, 1807

Olive: born October 16, 1811

Cynthia: born February 4, 1813

Loren: born July 3, 1814

Lois: born June 2, 1815

Thomas: born June 16, 1816

Mary: born April 28, 1819

William: born June 29, 1820

Braman: born September 16, 1821

Angeline: born May 24, 1823

Arabella Hayes: indentured to the Shakers as a child by her mother Sarah Hayes, Arabella is barely mentioned in the journals. However, she grows into a beautiful young woman who steals Loren's heart.

Derobigne Bennett: Derobigne--also known as DM--Bennett visited the New Lebanon Shakers when he was just fourteen, and made up his mind to stay. He grew up to play a prominent role as a "pharmacist" and also as a scribe during the Era of Manifestations. He eloped with Mary Wicks in 1846.

"CC" and "CM" and "DM" and "FSW" Chauncey Copley, Chauncey Miller and David Miller and Frederick Wicker: These men were among the leaders at the Watervliet Society. Diarists frequently referred to the Elders by their initials only; they more often spelled out the names of ordinary Brethren. Loren Wicks was variously referred to "L Wicks," "LJ Wicks," "Loren," "Lorin," or simply "LJ," or "LJW."

John M. Percey: a widowed farmer with several children who lived in Hoosick, and was a neighbor of the Van Hoosens (see below). Percey married Angeline Wicks, and they had one son together. His sister Sarah Percey executed Parmelia Wicks' will.

The Prentiss clan: Polly Wicks was the second-born of a very large family. Her parents, William and Mary (Watson) Prentice, had 12 living children, several of whom joined the Shakers. Polly, and her brothers Ephraim, Shubel and Sylvester all became Believers. Various cousins also joined, and one in particular, Oliver Prentiss, makes frequent appearances in the Watervliet journals. [Note: early in the 1800s this branch of the Prentice family changed the spelling to Prentiss. 1]

Garret and Delia Van Hoosen: this couple came and went from the Watervliet Shakers in the early 1830s. To begin with they showed promise as young Believers--both signed the Covenant-- but Garret and Delia were restless and conflicted in their commitment. Finally they "turned off" and left in 1835. They settled in Hoosick, where they accumulated some wealth, and were able to help out Parmelia Wicks and other Shaker friends, and where Garret became a leader in the local abolitionist movement.

Elder Seth Wells: Wells was a school teacher and school administrator in Albany before he joined the Shakers at Watervliet in 1798. He was an extremely devout Believer with a persuasive nature, which no doubt played a role when he convinced 19 members of his family (from Long Island) to convert in the early 1800s. Wells served as the leading educator for the whole of the eastern Shaker world, helping to found and guide schools in many communities.

Silas Wicks: Like Job, in the late 1700s Silas lived in the Troy area; later he established himself as a farmer in Reading, Steuben County, where Job re-located also in the early 1800s. There Silas Wicks owned property--including one slave--and seems to have been more successful than Job. How or even if Silas and Job were related is not clear.

Lydia Wicks: Probably a young widow, Lydia Wicks came and went more than once from Schaghticoke (across the river near Troy) to the Watervliet Shaker community during the 1820s and early 1830s with her three children: Eliza, Parmelia and Noah. She may have been a sister-in-law to Job.

Parmelia Wicks: Parmelia stayed with the WV Shakers even after her mother departed, and she showed promise as a young Sister until she started causing trouble among the teenage girls in the South Family early in 1837. She

7

was actually "removed" at that time. Parmelia soon relocated to Hoosick Falls (northeast of Troy), where she obtained a job as a housekeeper and companion to a Garrett and Delia Van Hoosen, who remained childless. Parmelia remained in touch with her Wicks cousins for many years. She never married, and died a wealthy woman. Her name was sometimes spelled Permilla or Pomelia.

The diarists, or "Scribes" ["R.B." " P.A.B." "I.N.Y." Initials are used in the following pages].

Over the years, many leading Shakers held official roles as journalists. These people were chosen for their writing abilities (both literally and figuratively). Some of the principle diarists are listed below, but there were others who kept daily records. Almost without exception, these documents tend to be dry recitations of daily life. Careful readings reveal occasional nuggets, however. A series of exclamation points typically indicates an 'AWFUL' event!!!

Rufus Bishop: Bishop was born in 1774, the year Mother Ann came from England. As a young convert, he came to Mother Lucy's attention and was appointed to a senior position in the Church Family in New Lebanon. Bishop traveled to and from the Watervliet Shaker community frequently. He was a copious writer, whose colorful accounts add great perspective to the Shaker story. His original record, which spans many decades--A *Daily Journal of Passing Events*--resides in the New York Public Library.

Phoebe Ann Buckingham and David Austin Buckingham: This sister and brother duo lived for many years in the Church Family in Watervliet. While most of the Shaker scribes were men whose accounts tended to be dry and straight-forward (Bishop's being an exception), Phoebe's entries often included sweet, personal observations of the natural world and the rhythm of life in her Shaker family. Phoebe and David also had a brother named Staunton, often referred to as "**SB**" in the journals.

Isaac Newton Youngs: Youngs grew up among the Shakers, having been brought to the Watervliet community as an infant. Later he moved to the New Lebanon community, where he wrote meticulously in his *"Domestic Journal of Daily Occurrences...Beginning January 1834."* The original journal resides in the New York State Library Manuscripts and Special Collections Division.

INTRODUCTION

A Young and Restless Nation

The following item appeared in newspapers around New York State, in January 1853, dateline Syracuse:

"A Shaker Marriage"

Quite an interesting marriage took place on the evening of the 12th, in Hawkley street in this city. It appears that two Shakers, a male and a female, belonging to a section between Schenectady and Troy, became enamored of each other, and determined to escape from a place where they were denied the privilege of entering into wedlock. They accordingly came here with flying speed, and soon had all the necessary preliminaries arranged for a marriage. The broad-brimmed hat and Shaker dress were taken from the man, and a fashionable suit of black given him in exchange, and the female arrayed in a neat fitting dress of the latest and most approved Parisian style. Thus rigged, they presented themselves before the Hymenial altar, and were made one flesh. A happier couple those in attendance never saw. The gentleman's name was L.J. Wicks and the lady's Rosetta Hays* and their ages respectively, 38 and 17. Rosetta is pronounced a lady of uncommon beauty of person, as well as cultivation of mind. After the marriage, the bridegroom related fully his experience as a Shaker, and the peculiar rites he was bound to obey. As part of his experience, he stated that he had never kissed a girl in his life, until he kissed Rosetta about forty-eight hours before their marriage. They started yesterday for Louisville, Ky., where they expect to spend their honeymoon." [1]

---

* the reporter made a small error here, the young bride's name was Arabella Hayes

The title would have caught the attention of contemporary readers, who knew enough about the controversial Shaker sect to recognize that its members practiced celibacy: "Shaker Marriage" was a contradiction in terms. The wide age difference between the groom and his young bride was less unusual in the mid 1800s than it would be today, but even so, this vivid little story resonates drama. The action--the hasty nuptials--apparently took place in a private home, whose is not known; L.J. Wicks' full name was Loren Job Wicks, and his sweet new partner in life was Arabella (not Rosetta) Hayes. The couple had both grown up in the bustling Shaker community in Watervliet, north of Albany.

Who were Loren and Arabella? How was it that these two lovers came rushing to the altar early in 1853? Why did they head to Louisville, Kentucky? What happened to them in the years that followed?

The origins of Loren's and Arabella's tale go back to the beginning of the 19th century, when the country was young and full of promise.

In the booming decades following the Revolution, the economy in New York State leapt forward, as land speculators and entrepreneurs of all sorts pushed into newly opened upstate regions. The result was that within a single generation--between 1790 and 1820--the state's population tripled, as thousands of families--mainly from New England-- migrated into the fertile and richly forested lands of western New York--along the Mohawk River, into the Finger Lakes Region, and toward the land that lay in the lee of the Great Lakes.

During this period New York's population mirrored that of the whole country, it was young: according to the 1820 census, the median age in the United States was 16 years, 7 months. (Today that figure has reached 38 years). In New York, as elsewhere, these young people were constantly on the move. The family of the famous Mormon prophet, Joseph Smith, is a good example. Between 1803 and 1815, the Smith family moved over ten times, around and about central Vermont, before finally migrating during the winter of 1816-1817 to the western region of New York. [2] This last move occurred soon after the famous "Frozen Summer" of 1816, when so many crops shriveled, and the consequences for farmers were devastating.

Joseph Smith once described himself as "a rough stone rolling," [3] and in many ways this term aptly describes the thousands of young and restless folk who sought to build new lives in new places throughout the first two decades of the nineteenth century. The world inhabited by these wanderers was a tumultuous place, filled with violence, both natural and man-made. People saw portents in the skies, feared their own evil ways, and often believed that the death of a loved one was an angry God punishing them. Early in the new century, an almost frenzied spiritual revival occurred in western Kentucky and eastern Ohio, where huge outdoor religious gatherings took place. From these super charged "holy happenings," itinerant preachers and the newly converted fanned out across the country to spread various interpretations of the gospels.

Perhaps nowhere did the religious enthusiasm exhibit more energy than in upstate New York, where people's restless urges were conveniently aided and abetted by the construction of the Erie Canal, which commenced in 1817, and was going strong by the 1820s. This remarkable engineering feat stimulated the economy: it is estimated that at one time over 50,000 people earned their living thanks to the new waterway [4]. Jobs and materials flowed along the new transportation link, along with gamblers, drinkers, roustabouts and salesmen of all manner of goods. This roiling mix of humanity presented a perfect invitation for those seeking to save souls. Joseph Smith, Charles Grandison Finney, John Humphrey Noyes and other powerful preachers all helped give rise to new faiths which spread westward in New York

State, through what later became known as "the Burned Over District," a vivid reference to the intense religious fires which burned hot and bright in the region. These social and religious dramas thrived and competed at a time when people in the country were seeking new opportunities. With the rapidly increasing population of New York State, potential converts were everywhere.

The Shaker experiment had commenced in the 1770's, in Watervliet, New York (also known as Niskayuna), but it wasn't until the early 1800s that membership in this new, odd Christian sect began to really expand. In the late 1700s, despite the fact that not many people were truly committed "Believers," their energy and productivity were extraordinary, mostly due to the determined and powerful personality of their leader, Ann Lee. "Mother Ann," the charismatic founder of the sect, had led her followers in an exodus from England in 1774, and her little ragtag group found cheap land to rent northwest of Albany within a couple of years of landing in the port of New York. It was from this swampy place-- located near what is now the Albany International Airport-- that Lee journeyed widely to preach her vision of the new faith, while her followers labored to drain the wetlands, hauling literally thousands of wheelbarrow loads of sand to create their new Zion.

Mother Ann's message presented a male and female Godhead of Christ, equal components of a perfect spirit; she emphasized the importance of confessing one's sins as the first essential step toward renouncing all carnal pleasures and seeking purity and perfection --"on earth as it is in heaven;" she demanded of her followers a willingness to surrender the self to the glory of the group--assuring them a new family within Christ's pure realm; and all were expected to practice peace and love in everyday life. These four basic tenets--Confession, Purity (Celibacy), Communal Living, and Pacifism--form the core principles of the faith.

By strict adherence to these guiding principles, one could experience salvation/perfection, and be accepted into the Covenant. The Shakers referred to themselves as "The United Society of Believers in Christ's Second Appearing," or more simply, "Believers."

Ann Lee had grown up in Manchester, England, the illiterate daughter of a blacksmith. Her world was one of poverty and turmoil. In her twenties she was married to a man named Abraham Standerin, who worked with her father. Little is known about Lee's youth: she evidently suffered through several pregnancies and deliveries, however the babies were either stillborn, or died in early infancy. Only one daughter appears in the record, and she died young. Perhaps it was Lee's failure to bear healthy children that persuaded her of the evils of human intercourse. She certainly railed against the carnal side of human nature.

At some point in her twenties, Lee became involved with a radical religious group--probably numbering no more than one or two dozen--who quickly drew attention to themselves for their confrontational style. These "Shaking Quakers" as they came to be called (for their jerking, violent movements during worship) began disrupting conventional church services. Ann was arrested for disturbing the peace, and imprisoned, and it was during one of her stints in the gaol that she experienced her first visions. Central to Lee's new religion was her impassioned experience of Christ's pure love, and her inspired vision of herself as the bride of Christ, sharing his purity. Lee soon emerged as the leader of the new sect, and she continued to experience powerful visions. In one vision, Lee imagined her little band crossing the ocean to the new world, where her flock could practice their new religion in peace.

The group that crossed the Atlantic in 1774 included Ann's brother, as well as her husband, with whom she no longer shared marital relations; and a small number of convinced

Believers. These few determined people labored at menial jobs in New York City before moving north to the upstate region. Somewhere along the way, Standerin drifted off, but the others stayed loyal, despite the fact that the immigrants once again ran afoul of the law. Even in the new world--where the Believers sought freedom of religion-- members of the sect fell under suspicion, particularly because they arrived just as the Revolution was breaking out. As newcomers from England who refused to bear arms for the Patriots' cause, they were inevitably accused of being Loyalists; and besides, their religious practices were rather strange.

In the early years, Lee's followers expressed their joy through ecstatic songs and swirling, stamping dancing; they spoke in tongues, and occasionally fainted when Christ's and "Mother's Love" transported them to a higher place. Lee was naturally suspicious of those in authority--the judges who had pounded their gavels while reading aloud her sentences-- and she eschewed the written word. Christ's message could be experienced by *anyone* who opened his/her soul and did not hold back their emotions. [Under later leadership the Shakers did write down their "Millennial Laws," and followers were encouraged to sign what had by then become a written Covenant, and it was at this time that the leaders commenced keeping meticulous records of the Society].

Mother Ann passed away in 1784, perhaps as a consequence of serious injuries sustained at the hands of mobs during her various missionary journeys. She was 45 years old, and had spent barely ten years in her new "Promised Land," after bringing her Believers from England. In the space of that time, this vibrant woman succeeded in planting the seeds of a remarkable new religious and social experiment.

Two very able leaders followed: Father Joseph Meacham and Mother Lucy Wright. Both were natural managers, and Mother Lucy in particular demonstrated a firm sense of direction. As the nineteenth century dawned, these adept

Shaker Heritage Society
Photo: Samantha Hall-Saladino

administrators saw to it that the faithful were "gathered" into new "Families" whose purpose was to construct heaven on earth. Land was cleared, fields dug over, buildings erected, and rules and regulations were promulgated and written down. The first carefully composed Covenant was created, an important document that laid out the principles of the religion, which all Believers were invited to sign, pledging their complete commitment to the Society.

In 1790 Father Joseph Meacham composed *"A Concise Statement of the Principles of the Only True Church of Christ"* which laid out the religious views of the Society, and this document was followed in 1808 by *"The Testimony of Christ's Second Appearing Containing a General Statement of All Things Pertaining to the Faith and Practice of the Church of God in This Latter-Day."* These tracts explained the Dogma, while within the Society, *"The Millennial Laws"* served as very specific guidelines for behavior.

In the opening years of the new century, more and more people joined the Shaker cause. The religion--the lifestyle--was demanding, but it teemed with energy: a Shaker community was a good setting for a restless individual to find a home, and make a life for himself. Even though members were expected to commit themselves utterly to the group-- to give up their own nuclear families in exchange for a large new Shaker Family, to forfeit their personal belongings to the Society, and to renounce the carnal life-- the rewards included the security of one's soul, and economic and social stability of a kind that many people lacked.

One early convert was a lively man named Issachar Bates, who spent some years roaming western Massachusetts and New York as a "New Light" itinerant preacher. Bates had a gift for music, and as a young man, he had led a pretty wild life. Precisely when he felt the power of this new religion is not known, but sometime in the early 1800s Bates confessed his sins, and moved into the newly expanding community at Watervliet, abandoning his wife and children. Although Bates urged his family to accompany him, initially they all refused. His wife Lovina was downcast and understandably felt betrayed. (Eventually Lovina and most of the Bates family *did* join the Watervliet Shakers, and several went on to hold important positions as teachers and musicians, following in Issachar's footsteps).

From his earliest days with the Shakers, Bates' gifts as a musician and preacher were recognized, and he was soon singled out to spread the word. Along with two other Shaker Brethren, Bates walked quite literally thousands of miles, criss crossing the Mid-west, in order to bring Mother Ann's gospel into the wilderness. These Shaker missionaries endured great physical hardships, including threats from wild animals and unruly mobs. They preached, argued, cajoled and sang with the people they met along the way. They were privileged to play a role in the American religious drama that became known as "The Second Great Awakening." Most importantly, they helped found and develop the western settlements of the Shaker world.

By 1820 there were 19 thriving Shaker villages spread out from Maine to New Hampshire, Massachusetts, New York, and into Ohio, Indiana and Kentucky, and with each passing year, the Society drew more members.

For all their quirks, the Shakers were practical people, and many of their efforts at building a better society still resonate today. They were progressive and equalitarian. In spite of the fact that the Believers lived by a strict set of rules, Shakers respected an individual's right to freedom of expression and religion. Above all, Shakers strove to reduce human suffering: and through hard work and clean living, they met this challenge to a large extent. Although Shaker communities were established apart from "the World's People," and were designed as Utopian cooperatives, Shakers were by no means isolated from, or ignorant of events in the society around them. They read and discussed news of the outside world, often finding their own society superior by contrast. Consider the following statement from an 1847 Shaker publication, meant for broad public dissemination (reworded slightly, this could well have served as a manifesto for the 2011 "Occupy Wall Street" movement or for Bernie Sanders' 2016 campaign):

> *The great inequality of rights and privileges which prevails so extensively throughout the world is a striking evidence of the importance of reformation of some kind. Who can view the unequal state of society, the overgrown wealth of a few, the abject poverty of the many, and not be convinced of this?...To see the luxurious state of the pampered rich, the oppression and destitution of the poor ...and the consequent bitter animosities and increasing collisions between the rich and poor, must suggest to every benevolent mind the indispensable necessity of some system of operation among [all people]*

*that will confer a much greater system of rights and priv-
ileges, both in person and property...[5]*

The Shaker system of beliefs and behaviors represented
a collective effort to share wealth and labor. Shaker villages
were productive places. From the outside looking in, this
lifestyle (excepting the demand for celibacy) made common
sense. It is no wonder that more and more seekers showed
up at the gates of Shaker communities. Late in 1824, among
those wanderers was the family of Job Wicks. Loren was Job's
first-born son. This is the story of Loren and his parents, and
his nine sisters and brothers who together sought refuge with
the Shakers. But it is more than that-- it is an American tale
of its time.

CHAPTER ONE

The Wicks Arrive At Watervliet

"There is a family of young Believers
come her [sic], 12 in number,
Their name is Wicks." [1]

Sometime during the summer of 1824, Job and Polly
Wicks left their children at home in Reading, Steuben
County, New York, and journeyed over one hundred miles to
the northeast to visit the Shaker community in Watervliet,
near Albany. Job may have been persuaded to investigate the
Society by some of his Wicks relations, who lived across the
Hudson River in Schaghticoke, not far from Troy. Perhaps
Polly communicated with some of her Prentiss relatives, a
number of whom had joined the Watervliet community during this period, and who were embracing the Shaker cause
with much enthusiasm. Polly's first cousins Oliver, Alice,
Channing, Angeline, and Laura all became Believers at some
point, as did her own brothers Ephraim, Shubel and Sylvester. The Prentiss Shaker connection seems to have been
a family affair, extending across generations during the first
half of the nineteenth century.

Polly's and Job's tenth child was a girl, who had been born
on May 24, 1823; the parents named her Angeline, likely after
the Prentiss cousin. It is possible that Polly and Job brought
little Angeline with them on the exploratory trip; or perhaps
the baby was left in the care of their oldest daughter Nancy. By

the summer of 1824 Nancy was almost 17 years old, already an adult by the standards of the day. She was a strong, good natured teenager, who was quite capable of minding her many siblings for a while. Caring for all those children had been her job for many years and she had able sisters, as well as her ten-year-old brother Loren. Loren was the oldest boy, tall and eager to help. Being without their parents for a few days was a challenge they could manage together.

As prospective converts, Polly and Job were treated warmly upon their arrival at the Watervliet community. The couple stayed with the South Family, which housed over 50 people, and which served as the "Gathering Order" for the Watervliet Shakers, the place where all first time visitors were welcomed. There, the Sisters and Brethren reached out--literally and figuratively--to make the newcomers feel at home. Job and Polly would have been invited to discuss details of their possible move with the Trustees. The Trustees--who oversaw all business transactions within each individual Shaker community--may have contributed a small allowance to Job, to help pay for the trip: such a large family represented a significant number of converts, so it was worth extending a beneficent hand to welcome them. Nevertheless, Polly and Job could not afford to stay for very long, but that didn't matter: they had plenty of time to discuss the issue during the lengthy ride home. Chances are, it didn't long for this poor and overworked couple to decide to move their large family into the secure world of the Shakers.

Job--who was aptly named--had not been having an easy time of it. In the 1820 census record for the Wicks, under the category "persons engaged in agriculture" there is a tick for "1"—this was Job, a lone farmer struggling to support a family of 10, including himself and his wife. In addition, between 1820 and 1824, two more children had arrived in the Wicks family: a fourth son they named Braman (possibly a family name), born in October 1821, and the baby Angeline.

By that fateful summer of 1824, Polly was 38 years old, the mother of ten living children: she must have been exhausted. Job was in his early 50s, still working long hours in his fields, struggling to raise enough crops to put food for twelve onto the table: he too must have felt used up. In addition, it was Job's misfortune to have so many daughters: the older children were girls: Nancy (17), Olive (13), Cynthia (12) and Lois (9), and although the arrival of Braman in 1821 meant there were now four boys, with the exception of Loren-- who had just turned 10--Job's sons were too little to help out much. Thomas was barely eight, little William turned four at the end of June, and Braman was not yet three.

Poor Job labored alone: the family did not have enough money to afford a hired man. The stark truth was. that by 1824 Job was destitute, and he was forced to look around for some solution to his family's dire straits. Whether he and his wife felt a spiritual calling toward the Shakers is not clear, but there can be no doubt that they were aware of the Society from public documents and discourse.

During the early decades of the 19th century there were many accounts in the press and elsewhere concerning the Shakers. There had been two prominent cases of women who railed against the Shakers: Mary Dyer and Eunice Chapman. Each of these mothers lost their children to the Shakers, when their husbands joined and in effect, "kidnapped" their children into the sect. Women of the period had no legal recourse, no ability to sue for custody: as a consequence, both Dyer and Chapman launched their own highly public and very personal PR campaigns against the Shakers, publishing salacious accounts of the perverse behaviors of what they considered to be a wayward group. [2] By contrast, others wrote positively about their experiences among the Shakers.

It was also during this period that the Shakers themselves mounted a spirited public defense of the Society, publishing various histories and witnesses' accounts of the Society's guiding principles. For practical reasons, it was around this time the Shaker leadership began using indentures-- proper legal contracts-- as a means of securing children into the community.

By the summer of 1824, with all the publicity swirling around the Shakers, as well as reports from various Prentiss and Wicks relatives, Polly and Job would have been well informed about the sect. Whatever awaited them, trying out life with the Shakers was a better alternative than facing another tough winter.

Possibly the family decided to wait for the harvest before moving. However, once the decision was made to depart from Reading, where Job and Polly had labored for more than 15 years, the matter of planning and packing probably didn't take too long, as the family simply didn't have much in the way of possessions. In any case, committing to the Shakers meant surrendering your personal world and sharing everything with the group. Soon enough, the family would be split up: they would move into large Shaker families, where their lives would change profoundly, as they all adjusted to a radically different lifestyle.

The late October journey must have been exciting for the younger children. Loren probably walked much of the way. Did he receive a pair of shoes for the long journey? It must have been a difficult and dreary trip, especially if the weather was cold and wet. Clattering along in a crowded wagon that bumped over packed dirt and corduroy roads, the ride must have seemed endless. Overnight, the family made do in the crowded, smelly quarters of wayside inns. In spite of the distance and the stress, Job and Polly prepared their brood for a big adventure: how exciting it would be, to encounter so many strangers who would welcome them into new "families." What drama awaited them all-- very soon now-- at the Great Gate leading into the Shaker village at Watervliet.

The record states that on 2 Nov, [1824] "Job and Family move into house at S.F. [South Family] East Lot formerly owned by Benjamin Youngs." [3]. Shortly after arriving, Job and Polly made confession--they "opened their minds"-- to the Elders, and members of the Wicks family were split up and assigned places in their new Shaker families. In the early 1820s, there were three established families at the Watervliet community--the Church Family, the South Family, and the West Family. These substantial groups numbered 70 to 100 people, who lived together (separated by sex), in neatly constructed small villages, each of which functioned with some degree of autonomy. Each family operated what amounted to a self-contained farm, with commensurate residences, barns and outbuildings.

The Shakers were prodigious builders, from their earliest days in what was then called Niskayuna. Long before the Wicks arrived, the Church Family--the heart of the Society--boasted numerous structures, including a Meeting House for worship, a substantial dwelling house, a large two- story building which housed a shoe-maker's shop, as well as room for the whip-maker, wheelwright, tailor, saddler & harness maker; in addition, there was a spin shop for the Sisters, a joiners shop, a wash house, an "old office," a tan house, the south barn, and a saw mill. An old log meeting house stood about 6 feet back from the new one. [4]

Ten year old Loren was assigned to the Church Family, and seems to have settled into his new environment well. His sister Cynthia was also welcomed into the Church Family, and within a relatively short time, the other children were assigned new families as well. Olive and Lois moved to the West Family: "Olive and Lois Weeks [sic] came to live with our family." [5] Nancy and Polly stayed in the South Family, with the youngest family members. It is not clear where the middle children (Thomas, Mary, William and Braman) were, but soon enough, they too were moved into new families.

The youngsters were given fresh clothing and, except for the toddler Angeline and little Braman, they immediately began to share in the routines of daily life--feeding the barn animals, mucking stalls, sweeping floors in the dwelling house, peeling and preparing vegetables in the large kitchen areas. All around them were the sounds of construction: hammers pounding and saws scraping--as well as the mooing and clucking of cows and chickens, the whir of the water wheel turning, along with the pounding of the millstone and--omnipresent--the soothing sounds of the wind and birds chirping. In addition, there was *music*: Sisters hummed familiar songs as they moved about their days, and the Brethren swung their tools to the whistled rhythm of dance tunes from Sunday's Meeting.

Music suffused all aspects of Shaker life, and religious services were community affairs, the time each week when members of all of the Families--who were otherwise some distance apart--gathered together for worship. On Sundays and for evening prayers, everyone who was able walked or rode to the large meeting house which was the centerpiece of the Church--or First--Family in every Shaker community. The members of the Society entered the Meeting House through separate doors--one for the Sisters and one for the Brethren--which led into the shoe rooms, where everyone changed into soft-soled shoes before proceeding into the large open space of worship. There, in long parallel lines or concentric circles of men alternating with women, the Believers meditated, and as they became inspired, they commenced singing and dancing for hours at a time, in loud and joyful praise of God and Mother Ann.

Mother Ann may have been illiterate, but she possessed a beautiful voice, whose power affected many early converts. It was through songs filled with vivid imagery that the gospel was conveyed. From the earliest days, Believers were spiritually transformed by this music: "[When] I saw Mother for the first time, she came singing into the room where I was sitting, and I felt an inward evidence that her singing was in the gift and power of God. She came and sat down by my side and put her hand upon my arm. Instantly I felt the power of God flow from her and run through my whole body." "When I arrived Mother Ann met me at the door and led me into the house...She sung very melodiously and appeared very beautiful. Her countenance appeared bright and shining, like an angel of glory, and she seemed to be overshadowed by the glory of God." [6]

Throughout Shaker history, singing and dancing were essential aspects of the Believers' spiritual lives, and many Shakers--both men and women--were inspired to compose hymns extolling Mother Ann and the Faith. Over the decades, literally hundreds of songs were written and circulated among Shaker communities. Elder Issachar Bates was among the most prolific composers, and other members of his family were also gifted musicians who helped spread the Shaker Gospel.

All those who joined the Shakers had--by committing themselves as true Believers--given up their personal possessions for the good of all. "It is an essential part of our religious belief, that all property should be held for the benefit and common use of the Society, and should be consecrated and devoted to the service of God...and that individual ownership of property is contrary to the examples of primitive Christian times, hostile to the spirit of religion, and injurious to the growth of the soul." [7]

The wealth of Shaker societies grew steadily in the first part of the 19th century, and much of the income derived from land holdings and other personal property provided by those who joined and thereby donated their worldly possessions to the Society. In many cases, such lands and goods were sold, and the resulting income provided the Trustees with the means to make the necessary purchases of materials such as glass, metal, building materials and other raw goods that the Shakers needed to continue growing their villages. Records show that during the first decades of the 19th century the construction of new dwelling houses and barns and storage sheds was constant throughout the seasons.

Although there is no doubt that many of those who joined the Society were sincerely seeking salvation, there is also evidence that many more who came were, likes the Wicks, simply hungry and cold. The sheer numbers of the needy were daunting. Not long after the Wicks arrived, the Elders at Watervliet prepared an interesting summary for the head Ministry at New Lebanon. The leaders there had apparently inquired about the numbers of dependents in each of the various Shaker sites.

This document provides a fascinating glimpse into how generous the Shakers were toward the poor and the infirm. The Society spent labor and cash to feed, clothe, and protect these indigents. In the matter of poor children there was the presumption that the youngsters would become life-long Believers. But adults who were in various ways vulnerable, injured or mentally unfit, were also offered protection, with no hope of any compensation to the community. This report is copied verbatim.

"In our estimate of the expense of supporting the aged and the infirm, who are unable to support themselves, we have omitted all such as ever brought any property of consequence into the Society, and all such as we consider have earned more than their living to their period--and also such as have children in the Society who ever possessed property. And in the estimate of poor children, we have omitted all such as are heirs of property, or who have parents that are able to support them.

Motives of delicacy, prevents us [sic] to have the names of those, who are supported by the charity of the Society, made public; but to give the Committee sufficient evidence, that our account is correct, we shall state to them the names and circumstances of such for their own satisfaction.

They are as follows:

Celinda Welch, a Molatres [sic: Mulatto], said to be 116 years of age, was formerly a slave--never possessed any property.

Ruth Turnner [sic] widow, aged 89 years--brought no property.

Gideon Cole, aged 70--has been from infirmity unable to perform any manual labor for several years.

Ralph Hodgson aged 70--from age and infirmity unable to support himself--brought no property.

Elizabeth Hodgson, aged 70--never able to support herself since she came into the Society--brought no property.

Hannah Salsbury[sic], deaf and dumb--aged 50.

Eunice Robins, aged 40-- taken [as] a poor child, is a lunatic subject to fits of delirium--unable to support herself--never had any property.

Tower Smith, a black man formerly a slave aged 70 years--taken from a poor house in Hudson.

Emily Owen, aged 18--taken from the Town--had her right hand ruined by being caught in a Cotton Machine.

<u>Poor children supported and educated:</u>

Amos McCalin, aged 10 years	Henry Chadwick, 10
Adaline Welch, aged 10	Mary Reed, aged 9
Lowry [sic] *Wicks, 10*	*Lois Wicks, 9*
Joseph Martin, 10	Lucy Snow, 9
Alonzo Owen, 9	Lucinda Snow, 9
Moses Sherman, 9	Emily Sheldon, 8
William Taylor, dumb, 9	Polly Chadwick, 8
George Conklin, 8	*Mary Wicks, 6*
Waldo Fuller, 8	Phebe Ann Taylor, 7
Thomas Wicks, 7	Polly Taylor, 6
Fenner Sheldin, 6	Ann Russel [sic?], 3

James Sheldin, 5	Emily Conckling, 7
William Wicks, 4	Weighty Sheldin, 2
Brayman [sic] Wicks, 3	**Angeline Wicks, 1**
	Alonzo Bound, 3 [8]

Twenty-nine children are listed, in addition to the nine injured and infirm adults: certainly this adds up to a large number of dependents. It can be inferred from the preamble stating that the children's parents were unable to provide for them, that Job and Polly arrived virtually empty-handed. The poor Wicks did not bring land or property to be consecrated: they simply brought 12 hungry mouths. [Nancy, Olive and Cynthia do not appear here, because they were teenagers, and already contributing to the community as young adults.]

Soon after this report was composed and delivered, the ever practical Watervliet Elders (no doubt with support from the Ministry in New Lebanon) decided to shift a number of the above named children to the New Lebanon community, in order to even out the numbers somewhat. Among those sent away were little Mary and Thomas Wicks, who were close in age, and may have appeared almost as twins. One can only imagine how these two small children felt, upon being uprooted yet again. It was probably cold and snowy early in 1825 when Mary and Thomas were conveyed by sleigh 30 miles to the east, and introduced once again to new environs. If only they had been able to bundle together under the same big blanket, and hold hands to console one another as they were borne away. It was not to be: the two little Wicks siblings were in fact transported to their new home on different dates, Thomas in January, and Mary on the 5th of February. "The ministry returns to Lebanon and takes Mary W. with them." [9] What did the future hold for the ten Wicks children?

CHAPTER TWO

The Wicks Settle In

"Put Your Hands to Work, and Your Hearts to God"
"Who Does his Best, Does Well"
"There is no dirt in Heaven, on Earth as it is in Heaven"
"It requires no Greater Effort to Speak a Kind Word, than an Unkind Word"

[A Sampling of Mother Ann's Exhortations]

Not much is known about the care of very young children among the Shakers during the early years. Mothers did arrive at the gates--often poor and/or having been abused--with babes in arms, and they were typically invited to stay for a while; but as a rule, the Shakers did not take in infants or toddlers. Following the negative publicity that resulted from the Eunice Chapman and Mary Dyer cases* the Society established new regulations to help control the comings and goings of children, and the practice of indenturing minors became the model. With a signed legal document, the Shakers had protection from courts, if and when an aggrieved parent or relative came to lay claim to a child living in the community.

Mothers and fathers arrived together, but more often singly, with youngsters in tow--the woman having been abandoned by her partner, the man having lost his wife in childbirth-- seeking a place for their little ones. There are dozens of indentures that provide evidence of the sad plight of unwed

---

*[see footnote 2 from Chapter One]

or widowed mothers, as well as fathers left with three, four or five children and no mother to care for them. These legal agreements--often signed with an "X" by the parent, and witnessed by Shaker Elder Brothers (rarely an Eldress) bear both poignant and practical testimony to the social realities of the times. The promise of a good, secure life with the Shakers was a far preferable alternative to begging in the streets; and for the Shakers there was the perennial hope that all these young dependents would grow up to become good and conscientious Believers.

By the mid-1820s, due to the large influx of children--some arriving with their families, as the Wicks did, others as the result of being indentured--the care of young people was becoming more regulated, and separate quarters for the children were gradually set up, sometimes called "The Boys Shop," and "The Girls Shop," or the "Children's Order." Children under the age of 10-12 boarded together and were minded by older Brothers and Sisters who presumably exhibited nurturing natures. In most cases these teachers/chaperones were happily inclined toward children--often they held such posts for many years--but the journals do recount instances of "revolving door" scenes, when inept, frustrated child handlers had to be replaced.

Among the Watervliet Shakers, for example (in later years) Brother Nehemiah White served for a long time as the caretaker of the boys, a position he seemed to cherish. There exists a charming photograph (albeit probably staged) of Brother Nehemiah, sitting in a field with his various young charges sitting near him and along the fence near-by. The image is almost languid, of boys and their chaperone, taking a mid-day summer break.

The Wicks family arrived some time before the concept of the "Children's Orders" had caught on in all Shaker communities, and it is not clear whether the new young charges lived in established separate quarters or not. The children's

Shaker Heritage Society (New York State Museum)

lives revolved around chores. The girls were put to work in the large, busy kitchens, where they helped prepare the huge amounts of food required to feed the 70 plus members of their respective Families. Each kitchen was run by a head cook, with numerous helpers assigned to specific tasks, from chopping to stove-top cooking to baking to the "sink girl," a lowly position; there were numerous food-related jobs that needed doing, all year long. Loren and his brothers mostly worked outdoors: mucking out the barns, and laboring in the fields where the pigs and chickens, cows and sheep needed constant care, the garden rows needed weeding, and fences needed mending.

During certain seasons, large work parties--consisting of Sisters as well as Brethren-- routinely went to the island in the Mohawk River where the Shakers grew fields of so-called "Broom Corn." This sorghum product was used in the manufacture of flat brooms. The Shakers originated the neat design of the flat broom, and men and boys worked in groups both outdoors and in the Brethren's Workshop to produce thousands of flat brooms. The sale of brooms was a main source of income for the Watervliet Shakers (along with medicinal herb products). Early on, Loren was taught how to select the small saplings needed for broom handles, and he was trained in the use of the lathe, the tool which produced the finely rounded spindle shape needed for a well balanced broom. Shaker boys handled a variety of tools from an early age, always under the careful tutelage of an experienced Brother. Everyone worked hard, every day, but for Loren, whose new life was so full of action and adventure, his many chores didn't seem like work at all: his brain and growing body thrived on all the challenges.

Also along the shores of the Mohawk River and on the island --"The River Farm" as it was called-- orchards grew, and the herds often roamed free. There are delightful diary entries describing happy days spent working and picnicking 'at the river.' From their earliest years, the children were taught to work with diligence and mindfulness: every task, no matter how small, represented a connection to God. Do your job with attention to detail, and you will grow that much closer to Heaven.

The children were well-trained, and by-and-large they were well treated. Although Shaker children were discouraged from having toys of any kind--personal possessions were frowned upon--their lives were by no means devoid of play. Songs and group activities were allowed, and there were many ways in which daily life could be entertaining, and chores could actually be fun-filled. Growing up Shaker was anything but boring.

All young people went to school, boys in the wintertime, and girls in the summertime. In the early years many Shakers were illiterate, and Mother Ann nursed a suspicion of the written word. However, as the communities drew more educated people, and during the years when Mother Lucy presided over the expansion of the Shaker world, it became clear that a basic education was essential for all Believers, and the first schools were organized. As with all forms of work, the enterprising Shakers set high standards in their classrooms. The younger Wicks were enrolled in the Shaker school, which was recognized as a bona fide member of School District Number 14 in Watervliet. There is little direct evidence of the degree of education each of the Wicks children received, although Angeline's handwriting--when she much later came of age and signed her name to the Covenant--is exquisite.

In January 1832, Elder Seth Wells, who served as school superintendent, gave a long and thoughtful discourse on education which was addressed to the Elders, Deacons, Brethren

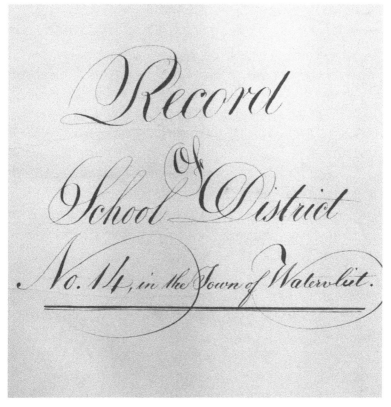

This fancy script is from the hand of David Austin Buckingham, who was the clerk of the Watervliet Shaker School for many years. "DAB" kept impeccable records. [New York State Library, Manuscripts and Special Collections]

and Sisters of the Society in Watervliet. Although in places his words sound pedantic and somewhat pompous, many of his observations about how children learn, and why education is important, still pertain today:

Beloved Friends,
...As the Society is in the habit of receiving children from the world, to be brought up under its care and protection, I consider the responsibility of believers for the faithful discharge of their duty towards such children to be very great...[for they must] occupy our places when we are laid to dust...

Example has a much more powerful influence upon the infant and youthful mind than precept---Children are creatures of imitation---They learn to speak and act by imitation. Their language is the language of imitation, and their actions are formed and brought into use by imitations.-- Even their ideas and opinions are the effects of imitations---and the Society and example of Brethren and Sisters with whom they are associated, constitute the source and foundation from whence all this imitation proceeds---What they see and hear their superiors say and do, they will say and do; and no admonition will prevent their following a bad example which daily is before their eyes & in their ears. How important then it is, that every Brother and Sisters who is in any way connected or associated with the children, should show forth good examples in conduct and conversation--One bad example in word or deed is liable to make a lasting impression on the mind of the child that hears or sees it...

...If these things are properly attended to, and every member of the family is careful to unite in the gift of encouraging and promoting the improvement of the children in the manner herein recommended, every good Believer will soon be sensible of the benefits resulting

from the school & feel an interest in its prosperity; and the children will then be in a fair way to be brought up under a blessing, & to become useful and profitable members of the Society.

This speech was presented at a meeting of the Trustees of School District No. 14, at the Trustees Office in Watervliet, January 27, 1832. It was "read and approved & ordered to be put in the School Records." [1]

What is remarkable about the Shaker school at Watervliet is how long it lasted, how thorough the record keeping was, and as the years went by, how many of the "World's" parents enrolled their children in the school, seeking Shaker--meaning high quality-- instruction. Today, in North Colonie--a large bedroom suburb north of Albany-- the secondary school proudly bears the name "Shaker High School," and remains a standard bearer for outstanding education, although there is no direct link between this school and its long-ago Shaker forebear.

According to the records, by the summer of 1829 Polly and eight of her children were still residing with the Shakers in Watervliet, while Mary and Thomas were growing up not far away, in the New Lebanon community. That year Nancy turned 22. Along with her mother, she had signed the Covenant, and had taken her place as a devoted, hard-working and respected Sister who in a few years would go on to hold an important position as a Deaconess. Sister Nancy and Sister Polly were both living in the South Family. In mid-1829, the other older Wicks girls were coming-of-age: Olive was not quite 18; Cynthia was 16, and Lois was 14 years old. The three sisters were by then wearing the special little white-veil caps which were a sign of womanhood among the Shakers. Little girls wore their hair bare and flowing free; as they aged they donned hair nets, and then as their bodies began to mature, young teens began wearing demure little cotton caps. Whether or not the donning of the cap was directly associated with the onset of menses is not clear (the Shakers were circumspect about such matters), but once a girl appeared in public in a cap, she was accepted as a mature young woman. [2]

The rest of the Wicks children were growing up as well: by 1829 Loren was a strapping 15 year-old-teenager, doing the work of a man. His aptitude for framing showed clearly as he helped out on construction projects, and he was also well versed in the broom industry. Loren's younger brother Thomas--still in New Lebanon-- was by now 13, and presumably taking on bigger tasks with his growing years. Mary was also coming of age at New Lebanon. Back in Watervliet, William and Braman were nine and eight, respectively, and little Angeline just seven. William and Braman were very much boys, full of restless energy.

The records are sparse, but it appears that during this period, Lois, Loren and Angeline all resided in the Church Family, which held the highest position in Shaker communities. William was likely in the South Family, and Braman and Olive resided in the West Family. By this time Cynthia (who was also known as "Cynthie" or "Cinthy") was likely spending time in the sick room, for she, along with her sisters Olive and Lois, was suffering from Tuberculosis.

Absent from the Wicks family in 1829 was Job. Job had apparently absorbed enough of the Shaker lifestyle to opt out sometime earlier: he is recorded as having left the South House on July 17, 1826 [3]. Job may have moved to nearby Schaghticoke, where there were other Wicks to whom he seems to have been related; or he may have moved back to the Otsego area. Job goes missing at this time.

Polly, the Wicks matriarch, seems to have taken well to her new life as a committed Believer. Information on Polly is scarce, but thanks to the Shakers' penchant for keeping records her birth and death dates are provided, and there exist a few other details about her life. Polly Wicks was born on February 28, 1786, in Deerfield, Massachusetts. She was the second child of William and Mary Prentice/Prentiss (the spelling of the last name changes at about this time). She died on September 29, 1863, and she is buried in the Shaker cemetery at Watervliet. Polly lived to be seventy-seven years old, a long life by the standards of the day. During her early years in the Society, Polly lived in the South Family. Almost all newcomers arrived into the South Family, which was known as the "gathering family." At least for the first few months after arriving, Polly had her little daughter Angeline close by her side; Angeline was probably still nursing, however there is virtually no evidence from this period of how the Shakers managed the care of babies and toddlers.

One imagines Polly settling in well as a Shaker Sister. Although she may have missed her middle children--when Thomas and Mary were sent off to New Lebanon early in 1825-- Polly would have been prepared for this fact of Shaker life: her other children were spread out as well, assigned to their new families. In her many years as a Shaker Sister, Polly herself moved from the South to the West families more than once. Deacons and Deaconesses made decisions about who would live in which family and in which room: as in any tight-knit group, issues of compatibility arose, and there were personality clashes. As mentioned in the last chapter, at any given time the Shakers bore the burden of caring for a number of mentally and physically infirm people. No doubt these individuals needed special attention, and there must have been a sharing of the load: those Sisters and Brothers who displayed a particular gift of patience (or who were worn out from a long stint) would have been assigned a new family now and then, to distribute the responsibilities fairly.

Polly's days were filled with work of all kinds. The Shakers deserve credit for seeing to it that people's jobs were rotated on a regular basis. In some cases a new job assignment would have been for a better "fit," but in most cases assignments were changed to relieve monotony and to grow people's skills. Chores tended to be gender specific, with women doing kitchen and general housework, while the men worked outdoors in the fields and barns. The following cryptic diary entries from an anonymous Memorandum book reveal interesting patterns in the daily life of the Sister author. The dates cover several years:

...A New Year you see...1823

J.4	*Elder B and Brother Freegift moves into the shop.*
18	*The Ministry comes here to see us [from New Lebanon]*
19	*I go to the kitchen to work*
May 22	*Freegift, Polly, Eliza and I go to painting the Meetinghouse and office windows*
June 2	*We finish painting office windows.*
Oct. 8	*I make ketchup*
9	*Chauncey paints his waggon*
11	*The Brethren & Sisters go to the river farm to pick apples*
12	*I make some more ketchup & butter*
19	*Finish gathering winter apples*
20	*Very snowy to day Sabbath*
December	
17	*We kill hogs, in the afternoon it snows like fun*
19	*We kill the beef for winter*

During the winter, the diarist mentions working on chair cushions, and spinning linen, good indoor jobs. Two of the Brethren "goes after mop yarn" and in the next little while the "Sisters goes to making mops." In three days, they finish 43 dozen mops. A good harvest of mops if ever there was one! [4]

Polly first entered her name in the Covenant of the South Family on "this sixth day of June, in the year of our Lord and Savior Jesus Christ, one thousand, eight hundred and thirty." At various times updated versions of the Covenant were composed, and Believers rededicated themselves by signing anew. Polly affirmed herself as a Believer once more on January 20, 1831.

The COVENANT or Constitution of the SECOND FAMILY
of the UNITED SOCIETY in Watervliet,
To Which is prefixed
A Brief Illustration of the principles upon which the
Covenant of the United Society are founded.
Come and let us join ourselves to the Lord in a perpetual
Covenant that shall not be forgotten. [6]

Polly, the mother of the large Wicks brood, seems to have found a degree of peace and security when she moved in with the Shakers, for what proved to be a long--albeit quiet, as far as the records reveal--life. Sadly, this was not to be the case for all of Wicks.

CHAPTER THREE

In Sickness and in Health

Part One: The White Plague

"The consumption appears to have made its way in among our young class of people and has laid claim to many of our most beloved and promising youth; this feels very grievous... but still it is a consolation that they have died in the faith of the gospel... [1]

There is a common--and largely correct--perception that Shaker communities were oases of clean, healthy living. Whether or not Mother Ann was actually obsessed with cleanliness--in a literal sense--is not entirely clear; what *is* known is that she worked ceaselessly to scour the "filth of sin" out of the souls she was seeking to save. Consequently, images of purity (spiritual cleanliness) abound in Shaker theology, maxims, and song. Most of the proverbs attributed to Mother Ann evolved some years after her death, but the sayings persisted, and provided practical and spiritual guidance for daily life.

One of Mother Ann's most famous precepts was "there is no dirt in Heaven; on Earth as it is in Heaven." Shaker Sisters and Brothers scrubbed clothes, scoured pots and pans, swept floors, brushed (and washed) animals, shook out rugs, shined shoes and boots, polished harnesses, pounded mattresses, and whitewashed walls-- in short, they strove in every way, every day, to create a world that was neat, orderly and *clean*...as they envisioned Heaven to be.

In addition to their habits of diligent cleanliness, Shakers ate very well. Mother Ann reportedly advised: "See that your victuals are prepared in good order, and on time, so that when the Brethren return from their labors in the fields, they can bless you and eat their food with thankfulness, without murmuring, and thereafter be able to worship in the beauty of holiness." [2] Shaker kitchens bustled with activity: labor was divided into very specific jobs, which helped promote more efficient food preparation and meal presentation. The Wicks daughters--as well as Polly--would have taken their turns at many different kitchen jobs over the years.

Each Family kitchen had to produce three meals a day for as many as 70 to 100 people, a considerable challenge. "The Shakers applied scientific methods to their cooking... working with vast [quantities] of food, they had to estimate and establish weights and measures and relative amounts." [3] They sought a balanced diet, and were far ahead of their time in their knowledge of nutrition and food values. In the words of Mary Whitcher, a Shaker Sister who lived in the Canterbury, New Hampshire community in the late 19th century, "The Shakers recognize that good food, properly prepared and well digested, is the basis of good health." [4]

As the steaming plates of food were brought in, the Sisters and Brethren filed into the dining room separately, and proceeded to separate tables, where they ate silently. The task of eating had a spiritual component: thankfulness to God, to Mother Ann--who was Christ's representative on earth--as well as to the Sisters and Brethren who had labored to produce the meal. One's business was to *enjoy* the experience, albeit in a quiet, meditative state of mind and body.

Not far away, just beyond where the meals were prepared by the hard-working kitchen staff, lay fertile fields, flocks of chicken, and herds of well-fed cows and sheep. The Shakers kept records of their food production, and the statistics are remarkable: an entry for October 1, 1835 states: "Since

March 15, the 1st Family at Watervliet from 24 cows made 2,000 lbs. of butter and 2500 lbs. of cheese." [5] In addition to their animals and vegetable fields and orchards, the Shakers grew acres of well-tended herb gardens. They used herbs as savory in their meals, as well as in the making of medicinal products. Early on, the Shakers began to mass-produce and sell herbs and seeds in packets, as well as in pill format in tins, and as elixirs in bottles. These products were universally respected for their quality. Shaker herbs and medicines--as well as packaged vegetable seeds--became huge money makers for the Society --in the order of tens of thousands of dollars. Particularly popular were their Medicinal Herb Catalogs

Over the years various Shaker communities--including the groups at Watervliet and New Lebanon-- focused particularly on the medicinal herb business.

Shakers led rich spiritual lives, and kept busy always. Community members ate hearty, nutritious food; they spent their days laboring in wholesome ways; their worship involved strenuous dancing and the emotional rewards of wonderful songs. The practice of celibacy meant that none of the women suffered illness or death from childbirth. Individuals were surrounded by many Brothers and Sisters who could provide emotional and practical support during difficult moments. With all of these healthy habits to guide them, it is no wonder that Shakers tended to live longer lives than the World's People. Perfection was their goal; however, even the pure minded, clean-living Shakers were not immune to disease and death.

Through-out the 1800s "consumption of the lungs" was the number one cause of death in the United States. Doctors sometimes called the disease "Pulmonary Phthisis," or simply "Phthisis" (pronounced "TIE-sis" or "THIGH-sis"). From the Greek, "phthisis" means "a dwindling or wasting away," an apt description of what happened to patients suffering

45

from the disease. Doctors and others struggled to find a cause, and they debated whether or not "lung fever" was contagious.

By the mid-1800s many people assumed crowding and unclean living conditions were the cause, but just as much credence was given to the idea that there was a hereditary component to the disease, and that those with a "weak disposition" were more vulnerable.

It was correctly observed that girls and women were more likely to suffer from consumption, although no one suggested that this might be because girls and women usually worked indoors--in kitchens or dormitories, for example--where they came into close contact with others who were already infected. Instead, the prevailing notion was that females-- the "weaker sex"-- naturally suffered from "weaker dispositions." During 19th century, the Romantic Poets found the pallor of those suffering to be somehow seductive, and they wrote melodramatic odes extolling the serene, noble natures of the victims. In his famous poem "Ode to a Nightingale," John Keats describes a youth (possibly his brother, possibly himself) who "grows pale, and spectre-thin, and dies." Like his mother before him, Keats died from tuberculosis. He was just 26. The pale, wane complexion of consumptives gave rise to the term "White Plague" as an occasional moniker for the disease.

It wasn't until 1882 that a German doctor named Robert Koch identified the micro-organism that caused the disease, which came to be called *"Mycobacterium Tuberculosis."* Remarkably, even after the identification of this deadly organism, it took much longer for the debate about how or if tuberculosis was contagious to be settled. Meanwhile, those who were coughing and sneezing millions of infected droplets into the air were unknowingly putting everyone nearby at high risk of contracting the disease. At long last, in the mid-20th century, the drug Streptomycin was developed as an effective antibiotic against the disease. Even today tuberculosis remains a leading cause of death worldwide, and is once more becoming an ominous threat, as powerful new strains of the bacteria show stubborn resistance to treatment.

The Shakers were very aware of the dangers of contagious disease. In the summer of 1832, when a cholera outbreak raged in upstate New York, the Watervliet Shaker Elders hastened to close the main gates to the village, and they quickly directed a self-imposed quarantine. It was precisely the right action to take, in order to protect the community from the epidemic, and in fact no one at Watervliet died from cholera. Ironically, *inside* their protected little world, dozens of Sisters and Brethren were already infected with tuberculosis, and with every cough, they helped spread the disease.

It is unlikely that any of the Wicks contracted tuberculosis during the years they resided in Reading, which was a small and isolated farming hamlet. People lived on remote farms, and life was carried on--quite literally--in the fresh air. Without exposure to the disease, none of the Wicks would have developed protective antibodies, and they would therefore have been vulnerable to infection when they moved into the close confines of their new Shaker community.

Shakers sometimes slept two to a bed. The Sisters typically worked in close quarters indoors, as they spun and cooked and cleaned and canned food together. The cooperative nature of the lifestyle meant that physical contact was often intimate. So it happened that--in spite of the preoccupation with cleanliness--Shaker communes were perfect breeding grounds for Mycobacterium Tuberculosis.

The most common form of the disease is pulmonary tuberculosis, which attacks the lungs, causing the victim to suffer a gradual loss of oxygen, as countless tiny lesions form (from the "tubercles"), slowly and relentlessly destroy lung tissue. As patients struggle to breathe, they cough and choke--often producing bloody sputum--and suffer fevers and debilitating night sweats.

The disease progresses gradually, and patients may experience one or more remissions (dormant phases), which may last for months or even years at a time. This episodic nature of the disease made it harder to identify: people would fall ill for a while, during which time they would run a fever, cough and lose weight, but then--as if by a miracle--they would undergo an almost complete recovery.

Although "consumption" was the prevailing form of the disease, lesions could form elsewhere in the body, particularly in the lymph nodes. No one associated the swelling of the neck with "lung fever," as the symptoms were quite different. The lymphatic form caused the lymph nodes to become enlarged and painful, and eventually the area began seeping, as nasty ulcers developed. This disease was called "scrofula," or more quaintly, "the King's Evil." The latter odd phrase evolved from the rumor that the touch of a royal hand on the evil swelling could produce a cure.

Among the Shakers, there was no talk of appealing to the king for a cure, although their journals are filled with entries describing both forms of tuberculosis. A Watervliet North Family journal entry from 1825 notes that some members were heading to the Church Family to the steaming mill, "to get cured of the consumpthing I expect." [6] Their destination was probably the Infirmary, known as the Second [Sick] House. Steaming treatments were a common treatment for lung fever. Some sanitariums developed elaborate piping systems--capable of delivering both hot and cold water treatments.

On Apr. 21st, 1838, *Amy Reed, having been confined in the 2. house about 7 weeks, came out and returned to her dwelling room. She is afflicted with a swelling in her neck.--king's evil, perhaps.* [7]

Amy may well have been treated with one of the many medicinal concoctions the Shakers were so expert at making. They were happy to share the recipes:

"King's Evil Plaster"

Take 2 oz. of Castle Soap, 2 oz. Rosin 2 oz. of Beeswax, 2 oz. Mutton Tallow and half a pint of rum. Shave up the soap and put all together in a jar. Cover close that steam get out [sic]. Set it on embers and let it set all night. Let the patient drink a tea made of Blue Violets and if the skin be broken make a wash of Blue Vitriol not very strong to wash it with when dressing it. [8]

Hopefully Sister Amy found some relief from an application of this plaster. In the meantime, Loren Wicks was probably suffering from Tuberculosis, along with many other members, including three of his sisters.

26 Sept. *"Lorin [Wicks] George Price and Nehemiah are confined with lung fever."* [9 **P.A.B.**]

End of December: *"Much sickness and infirmity among us. E. Ebenezer was confined for a week or more.--Luther had lung fever a fortnight or more.--* [10 **I.N.Y.**]

End of March: *"This has been a remarkable month with us. There has been much sickness, colds, & infirmities among us. 29 have been shut up, under medical treatment in the course of this month, i.e. 15 Brethren and 14 Sisters, besides others moreorless ailing. But a little has been done towards putting up firewood.*

Much sickness has also prevailed at the 2nd order this winter and month past--three or four have come near death's door.

Supplement to August: *"--Health in general about middling.--Luther confined near half the time --William Allen remains sickly--not wholly confined;--*

Dec (Sunday) 31: *"This day closes the year 1843.--It is now quite a time of colds and infirmities--there has scarcely been any cessation of sickness this fall.--"* [11 **I.N.Y.**]

John H. Murray summarized his research into Shaker death rates from tuberculosis in an article entitled "The White Plague in Utopia: Tuberculosis in Nineteenth Century Shakers Communes." His evidence reveals that in some years, the Shaker death rate from consumption was "nearly *double* the Worldly one;" [author's italics, 12] and in addition, the "death rate among Shakers fifteen to twenty-nine years old was... much higher than among all Shakers." [13] Young people in Shaker communities were being infected at a high rate, and they were dying at a high rate. Consider the case of young Milton Robinson, a consumptive in the South Union Kentucky community. Robinson grew ill on a voyage to New Orleans. While en route he was ordered from Philadelphia to New Lebanon, and the Elders there initially planned to send him back home. However, the poor young man was so weak, he "lived out his days weeding the herb garden and picking berries. He died at the age of 24 in the fall of 1832." [14]

Murray also vividly describes some of the remedies that the Shakers offered their patients, and he points out that many of the treatments actually made symptoms worse, especially those that caused vomiting or excessive sweating (loss of fluids). However, some treatments did ease the patient's condition, either literally or at least emotionally. Shaker Medicinal catalogs offered upwards of 150 plant/herbal concoctions for sale, many of which offered relief from coughs, scrofula, lung fever or consumption. Much of the Shakers' profits derived from 5 to 10 of their most popular products, which included Dr. Corbett's Shaker Sarsaparilla Syrup (made from wild dandelions); Cicuta (poison hemlock); Oil of Henbane (which served as both a narcotic and a sedative); Belladona ("Deadly Nightshade"); and the Opium Poppy. Prevailing opinion of the time still held that keeping the body's "humors" in balance was the key to good health, so purgatives were often administered in generous quantities to promote vomiting and diarrhea to help balance the humors. [15]

The journals offer scant testimony concerning the suffering of the young Wicks sisters. No doubt they became infected very soon after arriving in Watervliet, and over the next few years, they would have spent time in the sick house, even while they struggled to keep up with their assigned tasks in the kitchens, gardens or dwelling houses. Bedpans had to be emptied, rooms swept, meals prepared, candles set and snipped, stoves cleaned, wood collected...the jobs were endless and no doubt patients--except when they were in the sick room--wasted away more and more, especially if they were being treated with purgatives. None of the three Wicks girls lived to sign the Covenant, because none lived to be 21, the age of consent.

Olive, the second oldest daughter (after Nancy), was the first to die, on June 29, 1831. Seth Wells noted in the West Family journal, that poor Olive passed away "at about 10:30 PM. " [16] She went into the gentle embrace of an early summer night; Olive was 19 years, 8 months and 13 days old. Cynthia died only a few months later, on November 30, 1831. She was 18 years, 9 months, 26 days old. Last of the Wicks sisters to go was Lois, who died the following spring, on April 8, 1832. She was only 16 years, 10 months, 6 days old.

Olive Wicks left few personal possessions--Shakers were not allowed to "own" things--but one thing she would have treasured was a special copy of the Shaker hymnal *Millennial Praises*, which was inscribed to Olive from Lovina Bates, and passed on shortly before Lovina died in 1828 (probably of Tuberculosis). Lovina was the wife of the respected preacher/ missionary Issachar Bates, the lively fellow who spread the Shaker message so successfully during the early 1800s.

One hopes the Wicks girls died peacefully. What did their mother Polly feel, as she stood over her daughters' graves? She had lost three young adult children within less than a year. Those who attended the funerals raised their voices in lovely Shaker song, to grieve, but at the same time to celebrate the young person's journey to Heaven. Perhaps the hymn the mourners sang was one of the many composed by Brother Issachar Bates, "The Good Shepherd."

I am the living shepherd, and all my precious sheep
That stay within my pastures, I will forever keep
My life is not too precious, I freely lay it down,
To ransom all that's giv'n me, from wolves that prowl around. [17]

What were the private thoughts of the oldest Wicks daughter, Nancy, who had helped to raise her sisters? How long did it take for the news of their deaths to reach their father? Did Job experience any sense of guilt or responsibility, upon hearing the news of the premature passing of his teenage daughters? Sadly, the deaths of the Wicks sisters were so typical of the times--when *thousands* of young adults were succumbing to tuberculosis--that most people responded with a sense of acceptance: such deaths were part of God's plan.

Olive, Cynthia and Lois were laid to rest in the Shaker Cemetery at Watervliet, where their graves can still be seen today. Lives lost much too soon...who might they have become, in a different world and time?

Part Two

Gathering And Preparing Herbal Medicines

From their earliest days in Niskayuna, the Shakers gathered herbs, berries, roots and nuts which were used both for food and medicinal purposes. Like other early settlers, the Shakers learned from nearby Native Americans where to locate special wild plants, and how to apply them as medicines and salves. Although folk medicines were commonplace in the early 1800s, once the Shakers began marketing herbs, it didn't take long for the "World's People" to seek out Shaker medicines. People paid good money for them, and they got good worth. An early Shaker herb catalog printed in Albany listed over 120 herbs for sale, with advice on how to prepare the medicines.

The diarists frequently describe herb and berry gathering expeditions. The following excerpts come from Phoebe Ann Buckingham's wonderful journal, over several seasons: [1]

17 May   *Two brothers went for bloodroot; found it at Fonda's Ferry.*

14 June   *Go to Creiger's for black cherry bark; to Widow's Hills farm for crosswort for tea.*

27 June   *C. Miller and Daniel went to Saratoga for a load of cicuta.* This was *Conium Maculatum*, poison hemlock, one of the chief products of the Shakers. They recommended caution in using this powerful chemical, which was used to treat "tetanus, acute mania, rheumatism, and asthma."

28 July   *C. Copley and C. Miller went looking for lobelia and found none.*

16 Aug.   *C. Miller got some lobelia across the Mohawk River.*

Lobelia was also known as Wild/Indian Tobacco and Pukeweed, a rather graphic description of its effect. It was marketed as an "emetic," meaning it caused vomiting.

17 Aug.   *DAB and two others went to Van Schaick's Island for pennyroyal but did not get much.*

Pennyroyal or **Hedeoma Pulegiodes L.** is in the mint family. It was mostly used to promote perspiration and to incite menses.

18 Aug   *DAB and C. Miller went to Tymeson's for sweet bugle.*

Sweet bugle aka Bugleweed was "useful in phthisis, hemorrhage of the lungs, diabetes, and chronic diarrhea. It is a sedative and mildly narcotic."

22 Aug   *The botanists begin distilling peppermint and spearmint.*

15 Sept.   *C. Miller has finished making about 40 lb. stramonium extract.*

Datura Stramonium, aka "Jimsonweed" or "Thorn Apple" was "an energetic narcotic poison ... used as a substitute for opium and to prevent abortion, [as well as] for asthma, epilepsy, nervous affections, eye operations, and pain. One of the chief products and biggest money makers" for the Shakers. [2]

16 Sept. The physicians went to Tymeson's near Vischer's Ferry, for elderberries to make wine for medicine.

23 Sept. The botanist has made a large quantity of dandelion extract.

The scenes recounted above occurred in or near the Watervliet Shaker community. The Watervliet Shakers were among the first to publish "a Catalogue of Medicinal Plants and Vegetable Medicines," and to market herbal products on a large scale. However the business of gathering plants and preparing medicinal extracts was practiced in most Shaker settlements, where certain individuals gradually attained special training and knowledge of wild plants. These Brethren became known as "botanists" or "physicians," and they were rightly respected for their expertise. In effect, such individuals were *de facto* pharmacists, or chemists.

The sheer quantity of herbs the Shakers processed was extraordinary. Isaac Newton Youngs kept meticulous records, and enjoyed lists. At the close of 1836, he compiled the following table:

"For a comparison of a few years past I will state the quantity of roots and herbs put up:

YEAR	LBS.
1831	4381
1832	3462
1833	3565
1834	4610
1835	4496
1836	6030

Amount of past six years = 26,534 pounds.

This sort of on-going production is quite remarkable; and these figures do not include [from the year 1836 alone] *"900 lbs. of extract...and 36 dozen bottles of syrups put up."* [3 I.N.Y.]

During this period one young brother in the Church Family at New Lebanon , "DeRobign B," is often mentioned in the journals, working in the "Medical Department" and leading small groups into the surrounding countryside --including Sisters--to gather herbs and berries. Derobigne Bennett plays a central role in the Wicks story. However in the late 1830s and early 1840s he was merely a young adult-- one more rising member of the community, full of promise.

October 1842:

S. 22 The 2nd family made us a present of a load of pump-kins. Bartlet Wickersham, having been employed at the machine shop, left that quarter and went over to work with Derobigne Bt. at the herb business, preparing, paper-ing up [packaging] etc. Some rain.

July 1843 5th Nathan Williams and Derobign B. with 7 sisters, went after herbs for tea to Richmond Pond.

6th Edward F. Peter L. Derobign B and Bartlet W. and 5 sisters from here and 5 from the 2. Order went out west after elder flowers.

th. 13 Derobigne B. Betsy Cr. and Jane Bl went to Stockbridge after meadow sweet.

fr. 21 Derobigne & Bartlet finished grinding Cicuta for this sea-son. they had 14 load [sic], which yielded 742 gallons of pressed juice.

th27 Henry D.W. and Derobn B. Bart W. & 6 boys went out to the west part of our town after cherries. they got 5 1/4 bushels. [4 I.N.Y.]

All of these daily updates were composed by Isaac N. Youngs, in an amazing journal that this dutiful Shaker scribe kept over many years. Young's *"Domestic Journal of Daily Events"* is an extraordinarily vivid account of Shaker life in the Church Family at the New Lebanon community starting in 1834 and continuing for many decades. At the end of each month, Youngs wrote a carefully researched "supplement" which typically included a summary of the weather and activities and production of that period. The following notes are directly quoted, from August and September of 1843.

There has fallen, this month, about 7 1/2 inches of rain. The weather has been about medium for heat.--Haying has progressed slowly.--Health in general about middling.--Luther confined near half the time--William Allen remains sickly--not wholly confined;--Norman T. about the same.

... Note.---Our haying may be considered as finished,--There has been 124 horse loads from our common lots & 92 ox loads from the Pierce lot--254 loads in all. Daniel C. has worked with the boys, chiefly separate from the rest of the company, them haying, and they have cut and got in 20 h. loads from the Chamney lot above the north orchard. ..the help has been weaker at haying than common this year, owing to the work at the new barn.--Daniel Wood has been unable to take any burden in seeing to victuals & drink (which he has done for many years)--and the brthren have had to employ a boy or some one, the best way they can, or go without--

And sadly, early in the next year:

19. Mon. <u>William Allen departed this life this morning, not far from 2 O'clock, of Consumption, being in the 20th year of his age, since December last.</u> [Young's underlines, 5]

What is remarkable is that at any given time, a number of the Shakers would have been in the Sick House, confined with "lung fever" or scrofula or other ailments that left them too weak to work.

Those who could, carried on-- getting up early and striving every day to make a more perfect world. In autumn, as the days grew shorter, they got a bit of a break: on Friday October 20th, Youngs noted, *"Our time of rising alterd, from 5 to 1/2 p. 5. Breakfast at 7."* Rise and shine, no matter the weather, or who among them had passed on to be with the angels.

CHAPTER FOUR

Transformative Times:
The Era of Manifestations

"Yea, every one that did follow the commandments of God, and did
walk in obedience to his ordinances, did I guard and protect, did I shelter them with my holy wings: and I followed the obedient souls into
Canaan's happy land..."
[Mary Wicks, channeling an angel from God] [1]

As if the loss of so many people to consumption wasn't
enough, by the mid-1830s the Shakers were losing members to the world, as more and more (supposed) Believers
went away. Various issues of protocol were causing dissen-
sion: for example there was a lot of disagreement over the
new vegetarian "Graham Diet." The meat eaters wanted no
part of this fad. At the New Lebanon community, this matter
was a thorny one. *"Now, as a number have chosen to go back
to eat meat, the two north tables are devoted to that, and the
south one to vegetable food. Our experiments for simple food
doubtleys [doubtless] does some good, but it causes us considerable trouble."* [2 I.N.Y.] One can just imagine how the cooks
were complaining!

Figures in Shaker journals reveal that in spite of such
internal squabbles, the Believers worked as hard as ever,
with prodigious results. A sample from Isaac Newton
Young's end-of-the-year "Miscellaneous Items for 1836" is
quite delightful:

Work done by the Sisters: Two thousand palm leaf bonnets made for sale!

Young also includes a listing of the Family's stock: *1 bull, 10 oxen, 35 cows, 5 of them new milch. 10 heifers, 8 steers, 6 horses in the family, 2 for the ministry, 4 at the office, 2 colts (1 of them belonging to Job the hirling), 24 hogs and about 120 hens, 12 cats and 1 dog! No turkies. Thus we have 363 mouths to keep going besides our own 139. [502!]* [3]

Keeping this Shaker family going was a lot of work, but Young's gentle humor shows that there was room for play now and then.

Nevertheless, even while all this purposeful and productive work was being accomplished, the last of the original Shakers were dying, and direct connections to Mother Ann were being lost, quite literally. In August 1832 one Shaker diarist lamented that *"poor little Ann's old house is almost fall to pieces...[Today], assisted by the Second Family, we bury the earthly home of Ann, that dear little Saint."* [4]

This sweet sentiment was probably written by Elder Seth Wells, who had been an early and deeply committed Believer, along with many other members of his family. By the 1830s, almost fifty years had passed since Mother Ann's death, and too few of the younger generation shared the same religious fervency that had inspired the early converts. Although attendance on the Sabbath was often robust, and supplemented by outsiders--on Jan. 30, 1831, for example, *"100 Sleighs & Cutters of the World [were] at WV "* [5 R.B.]--more and more young people were questioning the authority of the leadership.

Additional pressure came from the steady stream of hungry and/or curious visitors who arrived almost daily at the gates of Shaker communities. Although the Society continued to welcome those who wished to call upon family members, and those who needed help otherwise, strict guidelines for guests were eventually established and posted. Still, visitors came in droves.

During the early 1830s, at Watervliet, the South Family--the Gathering Order--experienced almost ceaseless traffic from people coming and going. The following examples all come from the South Family journal: [6]

July 28, 1830: A man came from Albany to offer himself and his wife as candidates to save them from going to the poor house.

October 18, 1830 Charity Sanders (45) comes from Otsego Co. with children Harriet 11 and Laura 9.

December 20, 1830 William Richardson and woman came from Albany to join.

February 2, 1831 William Richardson goes to seek a privilege among the world.

And, following fast upon his heels...

February 3, 1831 Nancy Richardson goes, prays the Lord it is no sin to marry.

May 14, 1831 Jacob Simons comes from Troy; a poor man (David Camel) from : Liverpool; and Joseph Dixon all come.

May 15th Jacob Simon goes;

May 20th David Camel goes;

May 24th Joseph Dixon goes. He is a turnoff from Tyringham.

(This is a reference to another Shaker community; this fellow was evidently trying out different Shaker settlements, no doubt enjoying the hospitality he found in each place).

October 27, 1831 An unfortunate woman from Chautauqua comes. She had the misfortune to be born, be married, to have 8 children. She lost her husband and all the children but one. She is 34 years old.

October 28 She leaves.

November 3, 1831 A miserable woman and young one come from Manlius, leaving her drunken husband behind. Name of Mapes.

November 8 Mapes woman leaves

It is clear from these vivid entries that the Shakers dealt with a constant flow of poor and needy folk, who in some cases traveled great distances to seek refuge. Few stayed long: the demands of Shaker life were strict, and to make confession, live a celibate life, and work very hard every day in an extremely tight knit community meant too much sacrifice for most visitors. One wonders what happened to the poor abused women who moved on?

Meanwhile out in the Western Shaker settlements, the challenges presented by constant visitors and restless young people were compounded by bad weather and several years of poor harvests. Some of the villages in the Midwest were forced to make hard choices regarding closing and/or consolidating. Adding to these insults, in some communities trusted Brethren actually stole money and materials and scuttled off into The World. Perhaps these miscreants landed with a rude bump, and got their come-uppance in the outside world, for by the mid-1830s the country was careening toward what would become known as The Panic of 1837, which caused a major recession that lasted into the 1840s. Remarkably, much of the following pithy statement from Isaac Newton Youngs, from the end of January 1837, could have been recast in 2008:

It seems to be a time of much trouble abroad in the world. Great distress in commercial matters.--Serious difficulties in money affairs, numerous failures in banks; the whole banking system seems to be in consternation. The greater part of the banks having stopped paying specie and it is extremely difficult to get any hard money.

Factories are stopping work all about the country, public works such as railroads are obstructed & many are lying dormant--many thousands of workmen are thrown out of employment. Provisions are extremely high [priced] and a universal stagnation prevails. The newspapers are filled up with comments on banks, speculations, and money difficulties...It truly seems to be an uncommon time of distress & trouble in the world generally." [7 I.N.Y.]

In the face of all this tension--coming both from within and beyond their communities--it is no wonder that the Elders and Eldresses grew alarmed, and felt obliged to take some action. At Watervliet, in January 1837, commotion was brewing among some of the teenage girls, and the leadership intervened to staunch it. *"Permilla Wicks, having given little or no proof for her being a Believer & being found [to be] a ringleader of disorder & rebellion among the young females in the 2nd Family, was yesterday conveyed to the SF and to day carried to the world. Thus one rotten limb was cut off in hopes of saving others."* [8 R.B.]

It is not clear what mischief Parmelia was instigating--she was actually already in her early twenties at the time she was removed--but it is not hard to imagine a bunch of teenage girls generating disruptive gossip. The teenagers in the South Family seem to have been misbehaving for some time, possibly with a wink and a nod from their Elders. Blame fell upon Oliver Prentiss, who may have been insecure in his role as Elder, for the day after Parmelia is sent away, *" all of us went to the Second Family for the purpose of comforting and strengthening the faithful, & to labor to purge out the spirit of Rebellion, Herisy[sic] and Witchcraft which had O.P. fir [sic] its principal leader. "* [9 R.B.] Oliver Prentiss was a gifted but troubled man, and although he spent many years as an earnest Believer who held various leadership roles, he eventually departed in 1855 (Prentiss later re-entered the Society, when he was accepted into the New Lebanon group). [10]

In any case, during the early months of 1837, something was out-of-joint at Watervliet, and the Elders made a sincere effort to quash what they perceived to be troublesome elements. Meanwhile the heavy traffic flowing in-and-out of the community continued: on the 21st of May, 1837, the South Family complained that they had 22 mouths to feed, in addition to their own members. [11] It's no wonder young girls, who would have been working overtime in the kitchen, whined and complained!

It was into this air of anxiety and restlessness that a remarkable spiritual revival emerged among the Shakers, almost as if on angels' wings. In August of 1837 several young girls fell into trances and spoke in tongues and after they awakened, pronounced that they had communicated directly with Mother Ann and other holy figures. These girls--all in their early teens--proclaimed to have experienced powerful, transcendental visions. Afterwards they sang and described vividly special "gifts" presented by the holy spirits. Rufus Bishop described the opening stage of what became known as "The Era of Manifestations," on September 29th.

We went *"by request to see a young sister who was in a trance or vision last night and was taken again this morning while at breakfast and continued in that state until past noon. In all this time she appeared wholly insensible of all that took place among the living. Her name was Ann Mariah Goff, about 14 years. She and Elliet Gibbs were both in vision last night from 9 to 12. Some others in that family have been more or less exercised in the visions or trances, also some sisters at the SF, particularly Clarissa Shufelt and Elizabeth Abinatha."* [12 R.B.]

The Believers had always experienced their religion in deeply personal, very emotional ways, and at various times members had spoken in tongues, fainted and been transfixed for hours. However, over the years meetings for worship had evolved into more structured affairs, featuring predictable patterns involving rhythmic singing and shuffle dances with prescribed steps. In the summer of 1837 the ecstatic visions experienced by these young "Instruments"--as those channeling the heavenly gifts came to be called--had an immediate, transforming effect on the entire community.

The extraordinary revelations experienced by the girls soon began to possess older members at Watervliet, including men. On December 31st, Oliver Prentiss *"shook mightily and rolled about the meeting house floor."* The morning of the same day, Ann Mariah Goff *"was carried again into the spiritual world. She was carried out of the meeting house by two brothers and put into a sleigh but before she was out of sight she stood up and was under operations of the power of God."* [13 R.B.]

Ann Mariah and Clarissa Shufelt and other girls in the Watervliet group continued fainting and hallucinating into the New Year, and it wasn't long before the visions migrated to other Shaker communities. Over in New Lebanon, Mary Wicks is mentioned, on Saturday May 18, 1838: *"Mary Wicks was taken with shaking this afternoon, while opening her mind. She continued shaking & bowing all the time, both in meeting and out...Eleanor & Semantha had a wonderful time of shaking, bowing, talking & various exercises till past 11 ocl at night...others [as well were] considerably exercised."* [14 I.N.Y.]

More and more spirits were speaking through the Instruments, and often the heavenly guests were famous people from the past, ghosts of the past, as it were. It is important to realize that these visions were experienced as "real" to the Believers who were present during these mystical sessions. Rufus Bishop, a most enthusiastic Believer, was deeply affected and wrote often of the heavenly visitors in the prolific and lively journal he kept.

10 Nov. [1838]: "We had a powerful meeting tonight. We had a good many spirits attending with us, and Pontius Pilate with the rest. He has been a Believer for 365 years."

*10 Dec. "We had a wonderful meeting tonight. A great many
good spirits attended, among them George Washington
and Benjamin Franklin."*

*15 Dec. We had an extraordinary meeting tonight. Among the
various gifts, we had the gift of laughing." [15 R.B.]*

This is lovely to contemplate: a group of convinced, deeply
spiritual people, laughing and enjoying a convivial evening
with visitors from heaven. Here is another cheerful image,
from March 18th 1841: *"Mother Ann came into our meeting
and said I have been here through the meeting and with me are
come an innumerable company of angels and happified spirits which have assembled with you this night."* [16 R.B.] Who
could turn away from "happified spirits?"

As the revival lifted off, the Shakers continued to welcome
the World's People into their meetings. Over the years some
rather famous individuals had toured the Society: the Mar-
quis de Lafayette had visited Watervliet in 1784 (not long
after Mother Ann died), and Aaron Burr paid a call in the
1820s. In the spring of 1835 *" This afternoon a woman by the
name of Willard, who helps the female Seminary in Troy, came
out to Watervliet with her scholars, 97 females- who with the
choachemen [sic] &c. amounted to 110 or more--"* **[17 R.B]**
This was a huge invasion of strangers, perhaps Emma Willard brought the whole student population with her? Early in
1839 both Governor Seward and ex-governor Marcy dropped
in for meals and chats. [18 R.B.]

Extending hospitality to such illustrious guests made
practical sense: the Society needed to maintain good public
relations with those who held sway in the World.

On the 27th of February, 1839, Rufus Bishop described a
large party of visitors from the Legislature:

*27 of the Legislature attend meeting, plus a group from
Schenectady--total 39. The members from the Legislature
came into the dwelling house after the last meeting and*

visited the brethren and sisters in their rooms and had free conversation with them, especially the youth and children. They appeared wonderfully satisfied with what they had seen, heard and felt in our meeting and elsewhere, even to the shedding of tears. They saw and heard some of the wonderful works of God! But it is not likely that they saw the Angels that stood behind them in the windows & spread a covering over them, nor the golden chains that our good Fathers, William and James,** stretched between them and the Believers. But these, and many other wonderful things were seen by Such Believers as had their spiritual eyes open. [19 R.B.]

As the revival gained momentum, several of the Instruments found themselves capable, upon awakening, of producing finely detailed pictures of their heavenly experiences. These drawings were truly extraordinary. The paintings typically showed symbols of the spirit world, often in lovely pastel colors: trumpets and doves of peace and golden crowns and hearts and flowers and pillars and lamps, all painted in neat geometric patterns filled with Biblical meaning. Mary Wicks, along with Sementha Fairbanks, created gift drawings, and although Mary was not one of the more "famous" Instruments, she was certainly respected for her creativity and sincerity.

The Shakers studiously copied out all of the heavenly communications that were verbally conveyed by the visionaries. "A True Record of Sacred Communications; written by Divine Hand by the Mortal Hand of Chosen Instruments; at the Church at New Lebanon" includes a lengthy passage by Mary Wicks, when she channeled an angel named "Sa Ka Na la Vinda," bearing a message for the respected Eldress Ruth (heavenly gifts were frequently delivered through an Instrument for a particular person). [20]

** William and James were original Believers who had come from England with Mother Ann

"A Heart Gift from a Holy Angel" An example of a message brought to the Believers by an Instrument of God/Mother Ann [New York State Library, Manuscripts and Special Collections]

Mary's brother Loren Wicks also appeared as a bit player during the Era of Manifestations. As time went on, some of the spiritual messages included instructions for the Believers to choose special sites--sometimes up on a hill-- where the faithful should gather and focus their worship. New symbolic titles emerged--the Watervliet community adopted the special name "Wisdom's Valley," and the New Lebanon Church family took the name "Holy Mount"-- and the Believers commenced the practice of journeying to these "Mounts" in order to experience the spiritual world more intensely. Some communities constructed Fountain Stones at the Holy sites, or other special symbols.

Loren was present in on April 28, 1842 when a small butternut tree *"was planted on the spot of land marked by the Holy Angel of Light (now called the Holy Angel of Discernment) as being the central point of Wisdom's Valley, and one point is nearly due east from the center of our dwelling house. This tree was raised by a seed planted in the nursery in the year 1839. A number of the Brethren were present, viz. D. Miller, DAB, BS Youngs, FS Wicker, CW Brackett, W. Allen, L. Wicks and a number of boys down to 5 years. After the tree was planted, a short hymn was sung, 'The Healing Balm.' We also marched around the central point. Father Joseph's march was sung and played on special instruments."* [21]

Loren also served as an Instrument during the following December, when the Watervliet Church family was visited throughout the month by Indians and Africans. While in trances, various Believers channeled natives with names like "Lucy Wanapahoo" and "Fanny Wampoo." On December 9th, *"Loren Wicks became inspired. He said he was a chief from the Choctaw, his name was John Wampoo...Near all the younger part of the brethren and sisters were inspired..."* December 19. *"This afternoon fifteen of the brethren went in pursuit of the natives and I understand they found as many as six tribes, They were gone between two and three hours and when they returned they came hooting on their way."* On December 22...*"John Wampoo said he brought a wigwam filled with love."* [22 R.B.] One flinches at some of the stereotypical images of Indians and other "primitives" that flowed during the period, but such views prevailed across society, and in fact most Shakers held *favorable*--albeit rather romantic--views of Native Americans as "noble savages."

On yet another occasion Loren was observed sprinkling gold dust over a long, imaginary parchment covered in "hiragliphics" which was unfurled on the meetinghouse benches. Loren *"was forcibly brought forward with one hand over his eyes, while the other hand shook powerfully over the Roll as if sprinkling the Roll from end to end. Phebe A. Smith saw in his hand a box from which he shook a fine dust resembling gold all over the paper from end to end. Ann Buckingham saw an Angel & others had evidences of the hand of God in that work."* [23 **R.B.**]

Initially during the Era, those who were skeptical of these "gifts" were belittled and even persecuted, called out for being doubters. In the scene above, who's to say whether the gold dust was real? The pressure to conform overwhelmed logical thinking; and since when is logical thinking the rule? Among Believers, faith was key; Mother Ann's Gift of Love was omniscient. The collective desire to embrace and absorb her love was over-powering.

Throughout the late 1830's and early 1840's this intense spiritual revival seemed to grow in strength. Meeting journals are filled with detailed descriptions of the gifts brought by numerous Instruments. Here are some quotations from the early 1840's from the Watervliet Church Meeting Journal.

"27 Dec. While family was at breakfast Catherine Vedder, who waited on table, had a very solemn and expressive gift. She walked up and down the tables with her hands raised and sang a beautiful song."

10 Jan. [Near the close of the funeral of Nancy Wells] *"an inspired sister Emily Conkling told them that 'since we have been in meeting I saw Mother Lucy and our deceased sister come into the room and walk up and down the rows trying to get someone to speak for Nancy.' Mother Lucy brought Nancy to Emily and asked her to speak."* And at yet another funeral, Emily Conkling acts as an Instrument again when she announces "a present for Elder Sister which she had brought from Mother. [24]

Not only did the Instruments create lovely spirit drawings and deliver messages from angels; many of the manifestations took the form of music and dance. As already mentioned, from its earliest years, this new religion had been characterized by beautiful music and vigorous dances, physical expressions of joy which formed a central part of Shaker worship. During the revival, literally hundreds of new "gift songs" were shared by the Instruments, bringing deeper meaning to the services, as more and more Believers were swept away with visions from the heavenly sphere.

It was around this time--as the revival grew more and more intense--that many Meetings for worship were closed to the "World's People." Over the decades, members of the public had typically been welcomed at religious services, and although the "World's People" sat apart from the Believers (strictly separated by sex) many folks did journey, especially in pleasant weather, to observe the Shakers' peculiar dancing-swirling rites, and to enjoy the beautiful singing. In the early days of the revival, the public was still mostly welcome, and many came. One Sabbath day in June 1843 Rufus Bishop noted, " *it was judged we had nearly 100 spectators in the course of the day and they generally behaved with decorum.*" [25] However as the revival gained momentum, with more and more Believers channeling more and more spirits, there is evidence from the journals that the ceremonies at the Heavenly Mounts took on a serious and secretive tone, and Meetings were closed to the public.

For years the spirit messages flew through the air, almost literally. It was as if the early days of the religion--when ecstasy and mysticism predominated--were recreated. This was a *true revival*. The Era of Manifestations brought with it refreshing winds, yes indeed.

However, during this time of intense spiritualism, featuring young girls who were endowed with extraordinary power, it was almost inevitable that some of the Instruments began to single out particular people for special attention, not all of it positive. In the first stages of the revival, most prominent leaders had hailed the visionaries, and welcomed the visiting spirits, as shown by Rufus Bishop's eager descriptions in 1838. There can be no doubt that in some ways this unusual expression of visions and paranormal behavior was similar to other "contagious" group hysteria, such as the paroxysm that occurred in Salem, Massachusetts two centuries earlier. As Lawrence Foster has pointed out, in Salem the visions were put to evil ends, whereas during the Era of Manifestations, the Instruments proclaimed mostly positive, glorious visions that had the effect of uplifting the whole community. [26] Probably the Shaker Elders and Eldresses afforded the Instruments too much power: eventually there had to be a time of reckoning. Restlessness seems to have been contagious, and the leaders struggled with its consequences. *"I spent most of this day at the East Family with the Elders, and in labors with some of the young males who were in a dangerous situation."* [27 R.B.]

So it happened that numbers of young people were sent on their way, as Shaker leaders tightened up, and attempted to regain control of the situation. Emily Conkling, who seemed to like sharing gifts at funerals (and who had been with the Shakers since she was a child: her name appears on the list of poor dependents back in January 1825), was "removed." Many others who had played significant roles in the revival were either removed, or drifted away. And some--like Mary Wicks and Loren Wicks, as we shall see-- departed under dramatic circumstances.

In 1845 a new set of Millennial Laws was produced by the Bishopric in Mount Lebanon. These laws were designed to be a guide to daily life, but in this revised version, many were petty to the extreme, and were never really put into full effect. Nevertheless, the fact that the leadership deemed it necessary to produce this long set of new regulations--a major effort at behavior modification--indicates how seriously out-of-kilter some of the Shaker communities had grown.

By the late 1840's "skepticism and apathy within Shaker communities had already seriously undermined the effectiveness of the revival," which gradually wore itself out. [28]

The "Era of Manifestations" produced beautiful spirit drawings and lovely new harmonies and moments of true mysticism and personal transformation, but in the end it failed to help the Shakers rebound. During the ensuing decades their numbers continued to decline, and more and more of the records stated the stark truth, name-after-name: "gone," "went to the World."

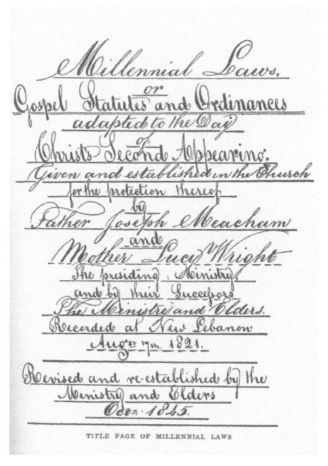

TITLE PAGE OF MILLENNIAL LAWS

[New York State Library, Manuscripts and Special Collections]

CHAPTER FIVE

Earthly Love

"Sisters must neither mend or set buttons on brethren's clothes when they have them on." [Millennial Laws, 1821/1845]

Life among the Shakers was highly regulated, and strict controls were placed on interaction between the sexes. The Millennial Laws of 1821 represented essential guidelines for daily living. In earlier years, in keeping with Mother Ann's suspicion of the written word, most theological and practical rules of conduct were primarily shared orally, when members "opened their minds," and through songs and aphorisms. However as time passed the rules of conduct were printed and periodically tweaked, as happened during the Era of Manifestations. Although not all of the rules were closely followed, the regulation above is a good example of how mindful the Elders had to be regarding actions between the young Brethren and Sisters.

To their credit, the Shaker leadership made sincere efforts to make sure all members were well informed of the essential principles of the Society. The need for a high quality education became more and more obvious, especially as the pressures to defend the Society against outside criticism grew. In 1831, the Second Family in Watervliet issued a new Covenant document, and the preamble emphasized this need for informed consent: any prospective member "shall previously have a fair opportunity to obtain a full, clear and explicit understanding of the object and design of the covenant, and of the obligations it enforms [sic]."

For the benefit of an illiterate member, this preamble goes on to say that the covenant must be read aloud "in the presence of two of the Deacons or acting Trustees of the Family." [1] Every effort was made to fully elucidate the terms and conditions of becoming a committed Believer.

The over-arching aim of the Shaker Millennial Gospel involved striving for a *pure life* in Christ's image. Hence the need for a full confession as a first step toward conversion. This process of "opening the mind"--which can be interpreted as *expanding* the mind--was often a profound experience. Many Believers--especially early on--describe their initial confession as a life-changing event. In effect, new Believers were truly "Born Again."

Sharing possessions... loving one another...seeking perfection through every action no matter how large or small... celebrating Mother Ann's Gospel through beautiful songs and dance...these were the holy rhythms of daily life that earnest Sisters and Brethren strove to maintain.

However, tugging against these efforts at pure behavior were, frankly, the *facts of life*: there were too many temptations, both within and beyond Shaker communities. The challenge of the leadership was to maintain order within the confines of their neatly designed, well-run, productive communal villages. Everyone was kept busy *all* the time; no one was afforded privacy; and from morning to night one's actions were carefully proscribed.

Loren Wicks and Arabella Hayes at Watervliet, and Loren's sister Mary and Derobigne Bennett at New Lebanon, all came of age under the constant watch of Elders and Eldresses who enforced the Millennial Rules.

"The Gospel of Christ's Second Appearing strictly forbids all private union between the two sexes in any case, place, or under any circumstance, indoors or out."

Brethren and Sisters must not work together, except on special occasions, and then by liberty of the Elders."

"Brethren and Sisters may not pass each other on the stairs."

"Brethren and Sisters may not go into each others apartments after evening meeting at night, except on some very needful occasion." (One wonders what such an occasion might be?)

"When Sisters walk out into the fields or to the barns or outbuildings, or even to the brethren's shops, there should be at least two in company; for it is considered improper for one sister to go alone on such occasions, unless by special liberty of their Elder Sisters."

"It is not allowable for brethren to go to Sisters shops to partake of melons, or fruits or nuts; neither should they go to the kitchen for that purpose, except at mealtime." [2]

Inevitably, young people chafed at these rules, and occasionally questioned the authority of the Elders and Eldresses. The young Wicks were normal in this respect.

Mary and Derobigne

Mary Wicks had arrived at the New Lebanon community in January 1825, when she was a little girl of six. In the following years, she went on to enjoy an uneventful and secure childhood in the Church Family, or First Order, and Mary grew up to be a conscientious and committed Believer, if evidence of her role as an Instrument during the Era of Manifestations is any indicator. Derobigne Bennett also played a role in the Era, as a scribe for the Church Family: he maintained the spiritual journal, a job he took very seriously. Derobigne--who later took to calling himself DM (for Derobigne Mortimer)--came to the Shakers as a young teenager, after a somewhat rocky childhood.

Bennett was born on December 23, 1818 in Springfield, New York, a small town at the northern end of Lake Otsego (in the Finger Lakes region, not too far from the Steuben County hamlet of Reading, where the Wicks had lived). Years after leaving the Shakers, DM composed his own autobiography, in which he spoke frankly--albeit stiffly, using the 3rd person voice-- about his early life: "Many homes have had their family trouble. The Bennett family had theirs. The father and mother were not congenial and did not live happily, and finally separated, the father leaving for another part of the state." [3] At the time of the break-up, Bennett's mother moved with her three children (DM had two sisters) to Cooperstown, at the southern end of Otsego Lake. Here, as a 10-year-old, Bennett landed a menial job to help support his family. Within a few years, he made a life-changing trip when he visited an uncle who lived in the Berkshires in western Massachusetts. This uncle had promised to help Derobigne train to become a doctor, but once he met his nephew, he decided DM was too small, for at the time the boy was but a "demure, slender lad, past fourteen and weighing but seventy pounds...[much too] small a specimen of which to manufacture a doctor." [4] It was determined that the young teen should wait a while: in order for the doctoring plan to take form, Derobigne *himself* needed to grow a better form.

Soon after arriving in the Berkshires, young Bennett had the opportunity to become acquainted with the Shakers in New Lebanon. His visit commenced on September 12, 1833, when he "was most kindly received in a family of some 75 genial, kind-hearted Brethren and Sisters who lived happily on the community plan with plenty around them on every side. The entire Society at that time numbered seven hundred persons. Everybody seemed agreeable and everything was lovely." [5] Imagine what a contrast the friendly, productive Shakers made, to the fractious, strained life that Bennett had so far lived. It didn't take the young teenager long to make up his mind to become a Believer: "After making a visit of ten days, the little fellow concluded he would like to become a Shaker and spend his days among such kind and happy people. Accordingly he confessed his sins (not a very black list at that time) " and was accepted into the New Lebanon community. [6] Both Derobigne and Mary spent their formative years in the Church Family.

In the decade following his conversion, DM thrived: he was well educated, and received training both in the medicinal herb business as well as shoe-making. By 1840, both Derobigne and Mary had taken their places as productive young adults, and it is possible to discern something about them from an interesting account compiled by the meticulous and loquacious Church Family journal writer, Isaac Newton Youngs. Youngs always presented his summaries in fancy script. [Note: the following is not inclusive].

A List of all of the names of those who resided in the Church on the first day of January. 1840

With their present age and their height attached.
Also, a hint of their occupation.

Name	Age	Height	Occupation
E. Ebenzer Bishop	71	5' 7 ½	Whip-brader [sic]
Br. Rufus Bishop	65	5' 7 ½	Taylor, Scribe, etc.
E.B. David Meacham	63	5' 10	Box Maker
Daniel Boler	35	5' 9 ¾	Box maker, prepares basket stuff, etc.
David Hofson [sic?]	80	5' 4	Maker of seed bags, etc. formerly a taylor [sic]
Francis Hocknell	74	5' 4	Makes pipe stems, formerly a hatter
Isaac N. Youngs	46	5' 8 ¼	Clockmaker-- Taylor
Derobign M. Bennet	**21**	**5' 5 7/8**	**Shoemaker** +herbalist

[written in pencil added later]

79

Youngs then gives the boys' names, adding, "These boys are mostly employed on the farm, and doing chores here and there, as occasion requires.--Getting in wood, etc." He goes on to list the Deacons (four of them), and states flatly, "The employment of the Deacons is better known than described." Youngs then moves on to the Sisters.

Sisters' Names			First Order
E. [Eldress]			
Ruth P. Landon	64	5' 5 ½	Various kinds of fine sewing
I. Henath [?] Clark	60	5' 5 ½	(both women did sewing)
Jeruah [?] Clark	84	5' 7 ½	Confined with infirmity
Molly Bennet	57 [67?]	5'0. ¼	Tayloress etc
Adazillah Potter	30	5' 2 ½	Caretaker of the girls
Hannah Ann Treadway	30	5' 1 ¾	Physician etc.
Mary Wicks	**20**	**5' 2 ½**	**Weaving, sewing**
Letsey Ann Bennett*	18	5' 4 ½	Tayloress

(DM's sister)

Next Youngs presents a long list of children, ranging in age from 5 to 14 with large brackets after their names, explaining: "These girls are employed in various ways, working here and there, as occasion requires, in the shops--workhouse kitchen, etc. Several of them brade a good deal of bonnet binding, etc etc. Learning to knit, sew, etc. Better understood than expressed.--"

Listed last are the Deaconesses, with their job description: "The duties of the Deaconess consists in regulating the affairs of the family, in the kitchen, at the wash-house, in the shops etc etc see to the providing of the clothes--garments, etc etc." Youngs follows with who lives in which room, and at last he concludes with a delightful caveat:

"NOTE: The heights of the brethren and sisters were taken as they are now, without any allowance for what they formerly were; and it is very uncertain what they measured just after

attaining their growth. There appears to be much difference in persons as to settling when old." [7 I.N.Y.]

Two facts concerning Derobigne and Mary stand out vividly here: one, they were both quite short, and two, there were very few young people in the Church Family Order. With so few members in their early twenties, it is no wonder Mary and Derobigne sought one another's company. How and when did they meet? Perhaps they went berry-picking together, or searching for herbs?

Shortly after Youngs compiled this summary, Derobigne was moved to the "Medical Department" where he resumed his old job (Bennett had earlier worked with herbs, before being pulled out for the shoe-making position). Back in the pharmacy, his responsibilities gradually expanded. In October 1842, young Bartlet Wickersham was moved from the machine shop to *"work with Derobigne Bt. at the herb business, preparing, papering up, etc."* These young men labored side-by-side, sorting and packaging herbs, and they also went on plant gathering trips--as well as to obtain other products--both near and far from the community. One can imagine the two men chatting on all manner of subjects as they strolled along, gathered herbs, and then returned home to sort and process their goods.

It probably came as no surprise to Derobigne when on Friday October 6th 1843, *"Bartlet Wickersham, having concluded to renounce our faith, went to the Office to stay until he can be taken to the R.R."* The custom for a departing member was to withdraw through a formal process which involved applying for dismissal from the Family. Those leaving were often given small sums of money and a few useful items to help them on their way. The Monday following Bartlet's move to the Office, *"Peter Long took Bartlet W. to the R.R.--on his way to Phila. to remain!"* [8 I.N.Y.]

Not long after Bartlet departed, *"Edward F. & Derobigne went to Albany on business and took with them Kimball &*

<u>*Charles Bruce*</u> *who chose rather to live among the world than with us.---"* On Wednesday the 13th <u>*"Edward and Derobigne returned*</u> [9. I.N.Y. Youngs' underlines] This journey was yet another opportunity for Derobigne to be out and about in the bigger world. It was also yet another instance of the steady drain of young people from the Society.

During the same early autumn when Derobigne and Bartlet worked together, Mary was assigned to assist with the girls. *"Today Mary Wicks went to the East house to take care of the girls, & Harriet Goodwin came from there and moved into N. 12."* [10 I.N.Y.] Often the caretakers of the girls were young women themselves, those who enjoyed being with little ones, and who likely developed "girl friend" relationships with the adolescent girls. Days would have been spent on housework, laundry, and kitchen chores, but there would have been opportunity to be outdoors in lovely weather and when the time came to bring in the harvests. During late July, August and September the fields and fresh air beckoned.

Describing life in the Watervliet Church Family, Phoebe Ann Buckingham's journal abounds with happy descriptions of this time of year:

July 14 ... Some of the Sisters goes after whortleburys [likely huckleberries]

July 17 10 of us goes after whortleburys we git 17 bushel[s].

July 19 Very beautiful weather, the bury fever runs very high

July 20 I am making Cherry Sause & some whortlebury ___?"

July 22 We have beautiful weather as ever I saw...

July 30 The berry fever is very high yet, we have beautiful weather

(Finally by the end of the month, Phoebe Ann figures out how to spell "berry"!)

July 31 Polly V. Ruth G. Lydia A and I go after berrys this fore-noon on the 40 acre lot, this afternoon Elder Sister and Polly goes to the river.

By September, apple picking had commenced:

Sept. 6 The Sisters begin to cut apples. The sweet sauce is fin-ished. Elizabeth F. Mary G and Nancy W[icks] goes to the S Fam. [11 P.A.B.]

Life was busy, but there were many happy days and social encounters to lighten the workload. At New Lebanon, the journals describe outdoor excursions involving both Breth-ren and Sisters, as well as boys and girls. In July 1843, a few months before young Bartlet departed, such parties sallied forth for days on end:

tu 4 Nathan Williams and Derobigne B with 7 sisters, went after herbs, for tea, to Richmond Pond.

6th Edward L. Peter L. Derobigne B and Bartle W. and 5 sisters from here, and 5 from the 2. Order went out west after elderflowers.--Nathan Williams also went out to the West hills, about 3 miles off--with 5 sisters, and got a large quantity of cross wort.--

Fr.7 A company of sisters went to the Pierce place, to cutting sage, with some brethren to help.

S.8 Nathan W. went again, with 5 aged sisters, to the west hills after tea, but were driven back by rain.

The fact that Youngs mentions "aged sisters" may imply that at least some of the other groups were made up primar-ily of younger folk.

th.13 Derobigne B, Betsy Cr and Jane Bl went to Stockbridge after meadowsweet. [12 I.N.Y.]

Ahh, happy afternoons spent gallivanting, going in different directions after different herbs and plants, with a different mix of people, what fun! Such occasions would have been carefully chaperoned, but there were still moments for lighthearted conversation and flirtation: a stolen look, a shy smile, a small shrug of a shoulder or the showing of an ankle... sensual and inviting moments, while at the same time secretive and subtle. How thrilling for a young person!

There can be no doubt that private communication was carried on among these young people; likely in the form of hastily written notes which were secretly dropped here and there. Although the rules stated that *"Brethren and sisters may not write for each other, nor to each other, without liberty from the Elders,"* both Derobigne and Mary had ready access to writing tools, and could easily have composed short messages to be delivered surreptitiously to one another and to their friends.

In addition, the young people at New Lebanon--indeed most members of the community--were well informed of changing social and economic conditions in the world outside the village gates. Shakers of this period--especially those who had grown up Shaker--were highly educated. Mary and Derobigne had been schooled in all manner of subjects--from grammar to the classics to mathematics and geography--and they were no doubt avid readers of newspapers.

By the 1840s, public debates swirled around a variety of controversial social issues, from the abolition of slavery, to the temperance cause and equal rights for women, to discussion of various religious experiments. The competition for souls remained lively in upstate New York, where preachers such as Grandison Finney in the so-called Burned Over District** drew hundreds to their revivals, and spiritual salvation was on the minds of many.

Starting in the late 1830s, a preacher named William Miller joined the fray. Miller was a farmer who lived on the border

---

**[The moniker "Burned Over District" came into use years later]

between New York and Vermont (only a few miles north of the Shaker village in New Lebanon). Miller gained many converts when he announced the forth-coming end of the world, and urged his followers to gather together and prepare for the Apocalypse. Through careful calculations based on Biblical texts, Miller pronounced that sometime soon (during 1843-1844) those who embraced the cause should prepare to meet Christ, while all others would perish and fall into eternal damnation. Thousands heeded Miller's dire warnings, and began surrendering their possessions in preparation for the end of the world. The Shakers observed the movement with bemused detachment: "_Millerism_ is running high in Albany & elsewhere about the country---great excitement--the world is about to be burnt up--some act upon the principle--sell off cheap, neglect concerns of life---some run crazy---some preaching to the rest & others laughing & ridiculing. etc etc" [13 I.N.Y.]

Of course, the world did _not_ end, even after Miller recalculated his dates and many of his acolytes gathered a second time, in high anticipation of the Apocalypse. When nothing happened, and Miller's followers were once again let down, this second anti-climax came to be known as "The Great Disappointment." [14] Interestingly, a number of the disillusioned turned to the Shakers for comfort-- Shaker theology also hailed Christ's Second Appearance--and various downcast "Millerites" sought spiritual and physical refuge at New Lebanon and Watervliet.

Another social and quasi-religious development during this period--smaller than the Miller movement, but equally controversial--involved the extraordinary "complex marriage" experiment started by John Humphrey Noyes in Oneida, New York. In the mid-1840s Noyes was inspired to create a Utopian society based on communal, shared-property values. Noyes admired the Shakers, and both he and his son Theodore visited the Shakers in Watervliet to learn more about their cooperative living arrangements. They were impressed: *"Their barns and arrangements of keeping cattle are much superior to any that we have seen, and exhibit great ingenuity of construction. Their washing room and laundry arrangements are models of neatness and convenience...They also have extensive arrangements for manufacturing extracts of various kinds, drying and packaging medicinal herbs and garden seeds. The manufacturing of brooms employs a number of hands. Their products sustain a high reputation in the market, and if you purchase a genuine Shaker article, you may be sure it will turn out to be what it is represented to be."* [15]

In the Oneida community, Noyes promoted a system of free love, in which members could form unions based on the open sharing of sexual partners. Of course this concept of "open marriage" was completely *opposite* the Shaker insistence on celibacy, but in other essential ways, the two cooperative societies had similar goals. Noyes disapproved of "possessive" behaviors, so exclusive relationships were discouraged. It is ironic that just as some members left the Shakers in order to wed and declare themselves legally bound as couples, so too did disillusioned members of the Oneida Harmony community depart, in order to marry and become conventional, monogamous couples. There were obvious ironies here.

The "Burned Over District" had also of course given rise to Joseph Smith, whose assassination made big headlines in the summer of 1844.

In July 1844: The Brethren had the reading of a newspaper this evening, which gave accounts of shocking riots in Philadelphia--of disastrous floods on the Mississippi, thro a great extent; tremendous loss of property, towns and villages inundated, lives lost---buildings swept off, etc etc---and also of news of the death of Joe' Smith, great trouble with the Mormons disturbances at Navoo, etc. -- [16 R.B.]

Imagine being a young Shaker, reading about such con-
troversial--and in some cases salacious--goings on in the outside world. Although free and open discussion of such subjects may have been discouraged by the Shaker Elders and
Eldresses, news of the bigger world couldn't be entirely sup-
pressed. DeRobigne Bennett describes a restless time: *"in the
Summer of 1846 a spirit of dissatisfaction and discontent over-
spread the minds of many of the young folks in the society, and
faith in the Shaker religion had lessened..."* [17]

Against this backdrop of social change--both within and
beyond their own Shaker community--Derobigne and Mary
fell in love. How and when the couple communicated is not
clear, but somehow they found moments to conspire, and by
early 1846, they were evolving a plan, along with Letsey Ann
Bennett (DeRobigne's sister) and John Allen, to depart to the
World. John's brother George also joined the group. Unquestionably this undertaking involved secret communications
with Betsey Bennett, DeRobigne's and Letsey's mother, who
still resided in Cooperstown, New York. Some years earlier,
Elizabeth Bennett had accompanied Letsey to New Lebanon,
and Mrs. Bennett had stayed a good while with the Shakers
before returning to her home near the shores of Otsego Lake.

When the young people bolted on September 12, 1846,
the news hit the Shaker community like a thunderclap. Isaac
Newton Young's was appalled:

*"An astonishing and awful event this day occurs, by the
sudden and unsuspecting absconding of four [of] our number, viz. John Allen, Derobigne Bennett, Mary Wicks & Letsey
Ann Bennett !!!! They had very privately concocted a plan,
agreed with a man at the pool to come with a carriage & take
them, which he did, coming to the gristmill, as far as the house
below the burrying ground [sic]. They 4 walked off not far
distant from each other, pretending to be going on some common business, no one suspected them, tho they were seen,
excepting in one or two cases, when too late..."* [18 I.N.Y.]

Rufus Bishop also wrote vividly of the event:

"We have a most shocking circumstance to record this day--namely 4 young people went from the 1st Order into the world!!! John Allen, Derobign Bennet, & his sister Letsey Ann, & Mary Wicks; this feels awful beyond description, and has caused many tears & such an occurence as this family never experienced before, since we began to gather together in the year 1787. But as they will not bear their crosses that must be separated, for Zion must be cleansed from sin & sinners." [19 R.B.] Bishop struggled to explain the absconding of such outstanding young people from the community. Surely they were duped in some way? The next day, September 12th, he stated that "poor Mary Wicks could hardly find words to express how awful it felt to her to lose her state of innocency which she had been brought up in. She said if someone could dig a hole in the ground & bury her therein, it would be heaven to her!!!" [20 R.B.]

The day after their departure, the young people were met by some of the Deacons who settled accounts with them; describing the scene Youngs maintained that *"some of them felt very uncomfortable."* [21 I.N.Y.] Bennett himself agrees, explaining (after-the-fact, many years later) that *"the parting from the home and friends of so many years was a severe trial. It seemed almost like 'pulling the heartstrings.' "* [22] It must indeed have been difficult for the young people to say goodbye. But their minds were made up. They were provided with a little travel money and their luggage was brought to them, and the quartet then left for Cooperstown, where they stayed with relatives. On October 19th both couples were married together in a simply ceremony, still wearing their plain Shaker clothes. [23]

Back in New Lebanon, the members of the community struggled to rationalize how such a shocking thing could occur: surely those who left were misguided? The sudden departure of such trusted, educated, productive and seemingly devoted Believers was a body blow to the Society. Within days there were other defections: on the 14th of the same month: *"Another sorrowful event occurs today--George Allen having decided to follow the late deserters to distruction [sic] was taken by Peter Long to the Rail R. Also Edward Fowler did out for Po' keepsie, & took with him Ambrose Cole from the 2 order, to leave him at Hudson, it being his choice, & he also being unfit to remain here."* Again , on the 18th of the same fate-filled month: *"One more Apostate: Stephen Baker, after being double minded a long while, has finally concluded to come out in his true character, & take a trip into his own way."* [24 I.N.Y.]

Clearly in some cases, those who left were not sincerely dedicated to the community; but the Bennett siblings and Mary Wicks and John and George Allen had been long time members and devoted Covenant Believers--their loss was keenly felt, for it was upon such young people that the future rested.

Youngs soon recovered his equanimity and resumed writing more calmly of daily events, but it seemed the loss of these vital members was a harbinger of things to come. The Shakers kept working and worshiping, laboring in the fields and kitchens, at meetings and on the Holy Mount, but perhaps something was out-of-joint. Hard times were approaching.

LOREN and ARABELLA

"Brethren and Sisters may not shake hands together."
[Millennial Laws, 1821/1845]

Loren was ten when his family came to the Watervliet Shakers in the fall of 1824. The journals do not speak of him until he comes of age, and as a teenager begins performing adult jobs. Shaker accounts rarely mention any details regarding children, other than by referring to them in groups, involved in menial tasks : "the girls picked apples at the river farm," "the boys went to help with the hoeing."

As he grew into manhood, Loren's name shows up more and more. He seems to have been capable of doing virtually anything, presumably in a good natured manner. By the time he reached his twenties, Loren was routinely going on trips with other trusted Brethren. January 1, 1835 : *Frederick and Loren starts for White Hall to meet SB and CC."* They were gone almost two weeks, and when they returned on the 12th, the diarist says; *Frederick and Lorin comes home quite pleased."* [1 P.A.B.] Evidently their trip was successful. The Watervliet and New Lebanon Shakers had various business interests in Washington County, including substantial lumbering operations.

Early in 1837, *"The floome to the mill burst to night JH and LW mend it."* Loren got up in the middle of the night, and he and Jesse Harwood responded to the emergency without complaining. [2 P.A.B.] In winter it was cold, and in summer it was hot, but the work went on. July 1838 was particularly sultry: on July 2nd, the mercury reached 100 by noon, and the next day, Phoebe Ann Buckingham commented *"another warm day, Loran Wickes [sic] begins to card [wool], the water to the Barn is failed, the tubs are dry & their [sic] is not enough for the Chickens."* [3 P.A.B.] In summer, when he had spare time, in addition to carding wool, Loren often did sundry painting jobs. Whether it was blisteringly hot or bitterly cold, Loren worked throughout the seasons without complaining.

Despite his steady and hard labors, Loren did not come to the particular attention of any of the Elders: in April 1839, when he went on a trip to NYC, he is mentioned by Rufus Bishop, who misspells his name: *"Also we [met] C. Crosman, Austin B. and Lary Wicks who had just returned from N. York &C."* [4 R.B.]

Loren was 28 years old when he helped finish work on

the new mill: 'It is 80 by 40 feet, well framed, no mistakes worth relating, went together nicely, altho the first building Loren Wicks framed." [5] Loren moved to the broom shop for a time, but mostly this strapping young man seems to have worked as a framer. On New Year's Day in 1846, "LJ Wicks put on the job on the west side of the new building." By the 24th of February, he had made a lot of progress: "LJ Wicks finished puting [sic] in the windows on the west side of the new building." It was a "cold and blustering" that day, poor Loren's hands must have been red and raw. On March 9th, Phoebe Ann Buckingham reported that "C Copley, LJ Wicks starts this morning on a journey to Buffalow [sic]. They went on the Rail Road." [6 P.A.B.] Wicks was traveling with a trusted older brother, the two probably went to sell or trade seed products or brooms. They returned six days later.

During the 1830s and 1840s, just as Loren was coming of age, New York State law commanded that every male citizen serve in the militia or pay a fine, and although there was a provision in the law for religious exemptions, there seem to have been constant tussles over the enforcement. For the Shakers--avowed pacifists--this law produced nothing but headaches, and there were numerous instances when the Believers' stand against the military authorities resulted in conflict.

In January 1832, fourteen Brethren were arrested by a martial named Dyer and his assistant, and all were locked up for two weeks. This group included several Believers from the South Family--among them Shubel and Sylvester Prentiss (Polly's brothers)-- along with five from the Church Family (it's possible Loren was in this group, he was just short of 18 years old), one from the North Family and two from the West Family. They were imprisoned for *non-performance of militia service, not withstanding that application was made by many respectable inhabitants of Albany for Executive Clemency; the Brethren remained in close confinement, in the putrid air of the common confinement of evil doers, for the full period of fourteen days."* [7] The Brethren were released and came back home on January 31st.

This was not the only occasion when the Shaker men folk were singled out by the local authorities. Over in New Lebanon, the leadership wrestled with the issue. On Monday the 3rd of April, 1837 "A meeting of the elders and trustees was held, to consult concerning the military affair. It was concluded to be best to take residence in the other state, and give the matter trial; and as it is likely that our enemies mean this year to push the matter on & try the law against us, it is likely that we will find out in the fall whether taking residence there will clear us or not." [8 I.N.Y.] At Watervliet, in September 1842 a number of the Brethren who were subject to militia service went to Troy to get a certificate from the doctor for their inability to serve. Loren was among this group (as were some of Polly Wicks' Prentiss relations), although what Loren's medical excuse was is not known. [9] The Shakers engaged in on-going debates with local authorities over the thorny issue of religious exclusion from military service.

In the summer of 1848, Loren went to work on the major building project of the season, the construction of a new Meeting House, which still stands today, and is the center point of the Shaker Heritage Society museum.

On the 27th of June, the main frame went up, and this event was hailed from afar in Rufus Bishop's Journal (which he kept at the New Lebanon community):

To day the society in Wisdom's Valley raised their new meetinghouse, they had a good day & good success; it took only about 12 hours; whereas we thought we should do very well to finish by daylight! It is 112 ft long and 52 wide, and looks very noble. The building has been mostly framed, Stone quarried and brought to the spot, the trenches dug & the foundation laid since we came to this place which was the first day of May. Oliver Prentice was chief carpenter &

A view of the Watervliet Church Family Meeting house, as it looks today. Loren helped to construct this building in 1848. [author's photo]

Jesse Harwood superintended the mason work, which was done by hired masons.

Loren was clearly one of the main carpenters on the job, but a greater number of experienced hands were needed, so the WV Brethren turned for help to the New Lebanon Brethren. On July 1st, Rufus Bishops again reported on the subject of the mighty new building:

> *Lorin & Justice returned home & tok [sic]with them from the First Order Isaac Youngs & Benjamin Gates, from the 2nd Order E. Brother Amos, from the 2d family Amos Bishop, from the North family George Wickersham & from Canaan James Wilson to work on the meetinghouse at Wisdoms Valley. Warm day- some distant thunder [10 R.B.]*

The challenge of rough and demanding physical labor was the lot of all Shaker men, and they often sustained nasty injuries from falls and saw accidents. Although there is no record of a specific injury to Loren while he worked on the Meeting House that summer, something may have happened to this sturdy carpenter, for on August 17th, 1848, " *Frederick took David Miller & Loren Wicks to Albany to take the Cars [RR Cars] for Canterbury, David to doctor [his] eyes, Loren for health, etc.*" [11 P.A.B.] It is likely that Loren was suffering from tuberculosis at this time, but apart from occasional bouts of "lung fever," he seems to have been quite fit, so perhaps this journey involved an injury of some kind. Hopefully Loren recovered fully within a short time.

On another occasion, Loren must have suffered miserably when he actually *walked,* a distance of 8 to 10 miles, all alone and in pain, to seek dental treatment: *"Nov. 7 Loren went to Albany in PM on foot to get his tooth pulled."* [12 P.A.B.] Poor fellow, what an unpleasant trip that must have been! In any case, by the time he was in his early thirties, even if he lacked a tooth or two, Loren was a strong and reliable Brother, trusted with major tasks, which often included traveling beyond the community with goods for sale. On November 29th, 1852 *"CM, Loren and Maynard started for NY. Frederic, SB & CC carried them to Albany & their loads."* This trio of Shaker Brethren were obviously off on a major journey, carrying a load of merchandise (brooms?) for sale in the big city. A few days later Loren returned. *"Tues. [Dec] 2nd Frederick Chaning and Eli went to Albany Loren came up from NY And came home with them."* [13 P.A.B.]

By this time Loren had considerable experience with how the outside world worked, and he must have entered middle age with a sense of self-confidence. How Loren managed to woo Arabella is not known, but the romance must have heated up fast, for Arabella was not even 18 when the couple absconded. Arabella was merely one of the "girls," albeit a very beautiful one. Her name never appears in any of the journals because generally the young people were not mentioned singly, unless they caused a problem, or were involved in a (personal) family crisis of some kind.

All of Arabella's life was lived with the Shakers. Her mother Sarah Hayes arrived at the Watervliet Shakers in the summer of 1839, when Arabella was just four years old (she was born on March 18, 1835). Sarah had come a long way--from the town of Lysander in Onondaga County--to give up her child, and it took her a while to make her decision, but on July 20th, 1839 the South Family journalist noted that *"Shubel [Prentiss] takes Sarah Hays and Betsy Springer to Albany to get their children bound.* [14] Sarah Ann Hayes seems to have been literate, for unlike many of the indentures--which are signed with an "X" by the parent-- this mother appears to have signed the document herself, in a neat and legible hand. Arabella was bound over to Elder Jesse Harwood, a senior leader in the community; F.S. Wicker and Shubel Prentiss (Polly's brother) signed as witnesses. The actual document was the standard issue indenture of the day, although there is an interesting addendum on the back: "Calvin Pepper a justice of the peace in and for the City of Albany in the County of Albany and State of New York Do certify that Abner Hayse [sic] the father of the Infant named in the within indenture has abandoned and neglected to provide for his family. Dated July 20th, 1839. [signed] Calvin Pepper Justice of the Peace" [15]

Sarah Hayes was not eager to depart from the Shakers: she actually stayed for several *years* after signing this indenture, living in the South Family. Perhaps her mother's heart was torn over her decision to bind her child over to the Shakers; perhaps she had a sincere interest in becoming a Believer. But Sarah finally made up her mind, and departed from the Shakers sometime in 1842. Although the records show that many parents dropped off children for short stays, an indenture was a serious, legal document, which involved

[New York State Library, Manuscripts and Special Collections]

an absolute farewell to one's child: there was no coming back next week with second thoughts. One wonders where Sarah went, after she left the grounds of the Watervliet village. Did she go on to bear other children?

Arabella--the girl with the exotic name-- grew up in almost ideal circumstances. If the newspaper article* describing her good looks and "cultivation of mind" is remotely true, Arabella was a well educated and articulate young woman of uncommon beauty. Although much older than his bride, in some ways Loren must have been "young" for his age; certainly he was innocent of some aspects of "the facts of life," having grown up sheltered among his Shaker brethren and sisters. However it is clear that over time Loren was afforded ample opportunity to venture outside the Watervliet settlement, and on these many trips, he no doubt received some exposure to how the "real world" worked.

By the time Loren and Arabella ran away early in 1853, his sister Mary Wicks was several years a bride, having married Derobigne back in 1846. The Bennetts had settled in Louisville. Clearly letters had been exchanged between the Wicks siblings, since the newlyweds set out for Kentucky on their honeymoon. But how/why Loren and Arabella went to Syracuse to marry is not known. Loren sometimes traveled to Schenectady on Shaker business, perhaps he made friends there who helped him? Perhaps someone from Cooperstown (friends of his brother-in-law) stood up for them? Perhaps Arabella's mother was present? As the newspaper article rightly observed, it was clearly quite an interesting marriage." [*see introduction] Back at the Church Family, Phoebe Ann Buckingham's journal relates the story from the Shaker side:

January 11 *Loren and Arabella Hays were among the missing at breakfast time it seems they took an early start for Syracuse. The Elders inform us that Josiah and Lydia [also]*

---

* see opening page, Introduction

hope to leave accordingly their things were brought to the Office an Inventory was taken of their things.

Wed. January 12 *There was an inventory taken of Loren's tools, his and Arabella's clothing [was] packed and ready when the word should come from them where to have them sent.*

On Saturday the 15th *CC and CM went to Schenectady to meet Loren at Givens Hotel (they got a letter yesterday to that effect) they met with him he was solemn but he behaved well he did not want to take the things as he had no place to store them at present but will write when he gets settled. [15 P.A.B.]*

The Shaker Trustees were generous with Loren and Arabella: Loren was given a good many tools, and $206.33 and Arabella received $41.00: not a lot of money, but enough to get them going in the world. [16]

The departures of Loren and Arabella, and Josiah and Lydia--like the earlier absconding from New Lebanon of Mary Wicks and her company--were a severe blow to the Shakers at Watervliet. The loss of four able-bodied and well educated young people diminished the community, not merely because it meant more work for those left behind, but also because the brain-drain mattered as well. Those remaining were aging, and although children were still being deposited into the arms of the Shakers, there were fewer and fewer individuals to care for newly arrived dependents; and the truth was that the odds were against any of those children growing up to become dedicated Believers.

CHAPTER SIX

The Wicks in the World

Part One: The Lost Boys

Thomas

Thomas is the most elusive of all of the Wicks. He was a little boy of eight when his family arrived at the Watervliet Shaker community in the fall of 1824. Poor Thomas barely had time to settle into his new home before he was summarily transferred to New Lebanon in January 1825. The shifting of children may have been a practical move on the part of the leadership, but it must have been traumatic for a small child. The Brethren and Sisters who cared for the boys and girls must have (by and large) enjoyed their little charges, but the job wasn't easy: virtually *all* of the children in Shaker villages had been uprooted at young ages. A large number were orphans, or had been bound over by their parents, as evidenced by the indentures. The very little ones no doubt wept and fussed when their mothers or fathers departed; some of the older children were likely sullen and withdrawn when they first moved in. Those with resilient natures may have had an easy time adjusting; but others may have misbehaved and caused all sorts of trouble. No doubt their caretakers knew how to distract little ones by keeping them busy in interesting ways: helping to care for the baby animals, practicing their letters, learning how to hoe in the gardens, and helping to pick produce.

In the winter of 1825 Thomas was probably a sad and lonely little boy. Whether he was a scamp we don't know; perhaps he *was* a trouble-maker. His years with the Shakers may have been tumultuous and unproductive ones, for in the end he left. One record states that Thomas Wicks "apostatized" on June 26, 1832. [1] Such a statement implies that Thomas- -just 16 years old--was bucking authority and not settling down to his Shaker business. Possibly Thomas moved to nearby Schaghticoke (not far from New Lebanon) where his father Job may have been living in the 1830s. One record says he went to Otsego to be with his father: Job's whereabouts at this time are not clear. What Thomas did under the tutelage of his father is not known. Thomas is the only Wicks who almost literally disappears into the mist. He *may* be the Thomas Wicks whose death was recorded on February 26, 1841 in Ashfield County Massachusetts. This Thomas Wicks was "a. 24," [aged 24] which matches precisely the age of "our" Thomas. [2] No cause of death is given, although it could be that Thomas succumbed to "the lung fever." There's a good chance he suffered from tuberculosis, but the cause of his death--and the circumstances of his short life--may never be known.

William

Next in age was William, who was born in June 1820 in Reading, before the family migrated from the Finger Lakes region. William was four when the family joined the Shakers, and perhaps--as we presume was the case with his brother- -William may not have been happy during his boyhood years among the Shakers. He is reported to have been "taken to his father in Otsego on January 21, 1833." [1] Job may not have been in Otsego at this time, but the Shaker diarist simply assumed that the absent father had returned to the area where the Wicks family had lived in 1824: Reading, in Steuben County, not that far from Otsego Lake. When William left the Shakers he was not quite thirteen years old; he was entering early manhood, by the standards of the day.

What happens next in William's life includes some contradictions and ultimately, tragedy. According to the *U.S. Army Register of Enlistments, 1798-1914*, William P. Wicks (born in "Redding," NY) presented himself in Albany, N.Y. on November 5th, 1834, and enlisted under the watchful eye of one Captain Morris. [2] The Albany location makes sense, if his father Job was then in near-by Schaghticoke, as some records indicate. Young William was described in the record as being 5' 6" tall, with grey eyes, brown hair, and a fair complexion. He was also listed as being 18 years old, and "a farmer." William Wicks supposedly served for three years in the Second Infantry, Company E, and was discharged on the 6th day of September, 1837, when his term of service was over. This record is interesting but cannot be entirely accurate because if William was born in 1820 (and there is no reason to believe he wasn't, considering the birth order and dates of the Wicks children), he would only have been *fourteen years old* in 1834, the year he enlisted. There is a note at the end of the record indicating that Wicks went on to re-enlist, in the 2nd Volunteer corps. Did he fudge his age to get into the army? If so, William must have appeared beyond his years, and/or Captain Morris did not have a very discerning eye after all.

Moving on to another record from the U.S. Army Register of Enlistments, on May 3rd, 1841, William P. Wicks, born in Reading, N.Y. enlisted with Captain Demick, in New York. By this time William--who gave his occupation as "soldier" had attained a height of 6' (he had quite literally grown up in the intervening years), had blue eyes, brown hair, and a light complexion. [3] He was supposedly 20 years old, which is/was correct (William would have been a month short of his 21st birthday). This stint was for five years, not three.

William served in the 1st Artillery, Company D as well as the
__ [illegible] Infantry Company C, and was reportedly discharged on the 24th of September, 1846.

However there were some bumps along the road, as William apparently deserted on the 11th of November 1841, and
was apprehended on April 5, 1842, "At New Orleans [illeg-
ible] Corporal." This little A.W.O.L. episode apparently didn't
cast too much of a blot on William's record, for in yet *another*
U.S. Army Register of Enlistments document William P.
Wicks, a "laborer" born in "Steuben" NY. (Reading was in
Steuben County) shows up to (re) enlist *again* on December
29, 1842 in Louisville, Kentucky, with a Lt. Woods presiding.
[4] William is on this occasion 5'11 1/4 inches tall (someone
was being extremely precise with measurements here), but
he has *black* eyes (maybe not so precise on this point), and is
still brown haired, with a fair complexion. He was assigned
to serve in the 6th Infantry, Company B.

William seems to have found a purpose in the army--this
despite spending his childhood among the Shakers, who were
avowed pacifists. In October 1846, William Wicks enlisted
once more, at which time he is correctly described as being
26 years old, 6 ft. tall, with blue eyes, brown hair and a fair
complexion. This is the right William, but alas poor soldier,
he is not destined for glory, for within less than a year, on
the 16th of July, 1847, William P. Wicks died of "fever, at the
mouth of the Rio Grande." [5] He had achieved the rank of
Sergeant, and was 27 years old.

William was no doubt a foot soldier in the United States
War with Mexico, which lasted from 1846 to 1848. Although
only about 1,500 active military personnel are estimated to
have lost their lives as a direct result of the war, many thousands more died from the various diseases that took hold
where poor sanitation persisted. Yellow fever was rife among
the troops, as well as cholera, measles, mumps and small-
pox, and of course dysentery. Perhaps William suffered from

a simple case of tonsillitis, which when untreated can be life-threatening. Whatever the cause of his death, young William met his end very far away from the home he had once shared with the gentle Shakers in Watervliet.

Braman

Braman was the "baby" boy, born in the autumn of 1821. He was barely three when the family arrived in Watervliet in the autumn of 1824, and like his sister Angeline, Braman had no memories of life before his Shaker family. Braman is rarely mentioned in the journals. He seems to have spent many years in the West Family, where he is listed in the 1842 census. In October of that year he made a big move from Watervliet to New Lebanon: *"Henry Bt. and Daniel Boler returned and brought with them Braman Wicks, who has come to reside here."* [1 I.N.Y.] Why Braman was transferred to a different Shaker community--after spending all of his formative years in Watervliet-- is unclear, although Rufus Bishop does say, on the 20th of the month, that *"This move was in obedience to Holy Mother & and our heavenly Parents;"* Braman may have been restless at the time. Perhaps Braman's skills as a joiner were needed at New Lebanon, for soon after arriving there, Braman was put to work in the furniture shop.

Over the years, different Shaker villages had developed reputations for special industries, and at New Lebanon, various Brethren were particularly respected for their fine cabinets, desks and chairs. As with other aspects of their daily lives, Believers strove to produce beautiful items. "Inspired and guided by a passionate devotion to the life of the spirit, the society's chair and furniture makers wrought into their work a sincerity...marked by great humility...in these labors the artistic coincided with the religious conscience, and in the end...utilitarianism [was] raised into the realm of undeniable charm and quiet and pure beauty." [2] Braman may not have devoted much spiritual capital to his handiwork, but it seems his skills as a joiner were put to good use. Like his older brother Loren, Braman was well trained, and a hard worker.

When he moved to New Lebanon late in 1842, Braman was 21 years old, strong and capable. The records show that besides working in the furniture shop, he labored on several essential projects at the Church Family. Braman helped build a portico on the east side of the machine shop, and assisted in rebuilding the "Tanners' great leaching vat." [3 I.N.Y.]. He was sent out to cut and haul timber from the Shaker lots in Washington County. Braman's muscle power was no doubt appreciated on such excursions.

Braman was also present on the Holy Mount after an incident in September 1843 when someone marred the sacred stone by writing "obsenity" on it. Braman and Brother Azariah went up to assess the damage. The very next day, *"Two of the Deacons, John W. and J.D. [John Dean?] went to the Mount to watch the sacred ground; they apprehended the youngster, whom they saw marking the stone, & caused him to come home with them. After mortifying him & making him promise he would come this week some time and pay the damage, they let him go. They said his name was Charles Cole."* [4 I.N.Y.] A few days later, Isaac Youngs went to the site to scour the stone.

Braman apparently developed a relationship with a fellow Shaker, whose name was Christiana Yons (perhaps Youns, a Dutch name). These two young people absconded together on the 24th of August, 1847. *"Braman Wicks & Christiana Yon, two flesh hunters, went to the world last night between 9 & 10 O'clock!"* [5 R.B.] Where they went and whether they traveled as a couple is unknown, but within a short time Braman headed south to be with his sister Mary and his brother-in-law Derobigne, who were still residing in Kentucky.

Sadly, barely a year after he went into the world, Braman passed away of typhoid fever, at the Bennett home on August

24, 1848. Braman seems to have been indisposed for some time before his death, because as far back as June, uncollected mail was waiting for him at the Louisville Post Office. [6] Why his sister and brother-in-law did not pick up Braman's mail, in the weeks leading up to his death, is a bit of a mystery--and how revealing it would be to know the contents of those missing letters!

The news of Braman's death soon reached the Shakers, for on September 4, 1848 Rufus Bishop wrote in his journal: *"To day we learn by News-paper that Braman Wicks dies of tiphus fever in Louisville, K.Y. the 24th [of August] at the residence of DeRobigne M. Bennet; only one year & one day from the time he left the church at New Lebanon! Short have been his sensual pleasures."* [7. R.B.] One can almost hear Bishop's sniff of disapproval: Braman got what he deserved.

Part Two: The "Truth Seeker(s)"

The four young adults--DeRobigne and Mary, John Allen and Letsey Ann--who had absconded from New Lebanon in September 1846 were certainly jolted by the challenge of making a living beyond the protected bounds of their Shaker village. Through an acquaintance, the men had managed to secure jobs in a nursery business run by one Mr. Byram, in Brandenburg, Kentucky. This is where the newly-weds headed--along with George Allen, John Allen's brother--in October 1846. In DeRobigne's slightly stiff, third person account: "It was a most uninviting locality. It was in the days of slavery, and as all parties from the north were viewed with suspicion, the reception the five met with was anything but agreeable. They found also that the representations made by Byram could not be fulfilled. [With] this unpleasant fact staring them in the face, and just as winter was coming on, and wholly unacquainted as they were with the ways of the world, Bennet and his wife decided to leave that place and repair to Louisville. Here he soon obtained a clerkship in a drug store, where he remained a better part of a year. They commenced housekeeping upon the most frugal and economic plan, and saved every cent they could." [1]

The young couple endured lean times; the bitter realities of being poor with no one to lean upon must have been a challenge to their relationship. They seem to have emerged stronger as a couple, in spite of (or perhaps as the consequence of) losing a child at birth, surely a huge sadness to them both. [2] Derobigne boasts in his autobiography of being a successful pharmacist, and he proudly hung up a billboard stating he was a Doctor. Perhaps Bennett did make a good living for a while, but the poor ex-Shaker had absolutely no financial acumen: after a series of disastrous business ventures, he seems to have lost virtually everything. Bennett's various schemes involved insurance stock, mining in Sonora, petroleum and mineral lands, a chromo-lithography business, a "bed-spring" investment, and finally a brick business in Long Island. [3] These investments all failed miserably.

Mary and Derobigne eventually moved to Paris, Illinois, where Bennett once again advertised himself as a doctor and sold medicines. At some point he experimented with the seed business, inspired by his sister Letsey Ann and his brother-in-law John Allen, who were by now running a successful plant nursery based in Rochester (New York), which also had outlets in the mid-west. Both couples had some degree of success with businesses closely related to their Shaker training. However, DM and Mary continued to flounder financially, and in the 1870 census, Mary Bennett is actually counted back east in Hoosick, New York, where she was a resident in her sister Angeline [Wicks] Percey's home, and was listed as a "domestic servant." She was 51 years old at the time, and still performing menial labor. Clearly, DM and Mary were experiencing hard times [Interestingly, in this same 1870 census, Mary Wicks Bennett was also counted as resident in Rochester, New York. The Bennett household there listed three people: DM as well as his wife and mother--Mary appears to have been counted twice].

While in Paris, Illinois, DM engaged in a heated debate with some local clergymen on the subject of prayer. During this period, Mary and Derobigne seem to have been evolving their perspectives on religion. In response to his confrontation with the churchmen, Bennett tried to get a local paper to print his rebuttal, but he was refused space for his opinion. This rankled, so Bennett took things into his own hands and decided to start his own journal. He and Mary considered many titles for the new enterprise, and eventually they settled on one of Mary's suggestions, *"The Truth Seeker."* [4] With the inauguration of this publication, Derobigne at last found a fitting vocation--his calling, in fact--and although initial sales were lackluster, the couple eventually relocated the journal--and themselves--to New York City, where *"The Truth Seeker"* found both readers and financial support, as well as fame and notoriety.

If *"The Truth Seeker"* had a muse, his name was Thomas Paine, and his vector was *"The Age of Reason,"* which created a huge stir when it was first published in 1794. The public remembered Tom Paine for his pithy pamphlet *"Common Sense,"* which had helped ignite the American Revolution. But Paine's patriotic reputation was undone with the publication of *"The Age of Reason,"* which challenged the truth of the Bible, and called for one's right to assert *no* religion. To most Americans--then, and even today--this was considered heretical, and ministers railed against Paine from their pulpits. Here and there, a few brave and independent people accepted Paine's argument, and these iconoclasts became known as "Freethinkers." When Derobigne Mortimer Bennett encountered Tom Paine's writings, his life changed.

As children brought up in a strict Shaker environment, Mary and Derobigne would not have considered life without a God. Both of them were guided by their faith, and both were inspired participants in the ecstatic revival known as "The Era of Manifestations." Belief in Mother Ann's dual Godhead would have been deeply engrained. In religious terms, even when Mary and Derobigne first became "ex-Believers," they remained devout Christians.

However, part of Shaker life involved reading and reflecting on the bigger world. Each week, in Union Meeting, hymns were sung and religious as well as other matters were discussed. In many respects Shakers were lively and open-minded people. Intellectual curiosity was not frowned upon, although straying from the path of righteousness was of course sinful.

Tom Paine's writings offered Derobigne a chance to re-examine his own thinking, and the person who emerged had come a long way from his Shaker roots. Some essential Shaker tenets still persisted in DM's heart--both Mary and Derobigne were ardent Spiritualists--but when Bennett proclaimed himself to be a "deist," this amounted to a complete rejection of the Believers' Dogma.

Toiling to make a living, traveling from place to place and state to state, the Bennetts must have been an interesting couple: two people with active minds, and an eagerness to explore the world. They were both readers and critical thinkers, thoroughly informed about current events and matters of philosophy and politics: they were genuine "Truth Seekers."

Like his fore bearer Tom Paine, DM's heretical views--his insistence on his own right to be an "infidel" (as Freethinkers were derisively called)--got him into hot water. As support for *"The Truth Seeker"* grew, so did Bennett's reputation. Through the pages of his journal, he championed the rights of all men (and women) to follow the dictates of science, for "this class of men discard mythical fables and mystical legends, and base their investigations and their conclusions upon the facts which the closest scrutiny fully establishes." [5]

Bennett's journal published articles discussing everything from universal suffrage to birth control to the latest inventions in technology and communications. Bennett pushed the envelope, and because he challenged conventional ways of thinking, he came into conflict with those in power, particularly those who fashioned themselves to be the custodians of public morals. No one stood taller in the Moral Police Brigade than Anthony Comstock, who was the lead Special Agent for the United States Post Office. As the head of the New York Society for the Suppression of Vice, Comstock spear-headed a successful effort to get the United States Congress to pass a law forbidding the transport of obscene materials through the mails. This law--known as "The Comstock Law"--provided the moral police with broad grounds for harassment, and Comstock went after offenders with puffed up, self-righteous authority. Bennett's journal fell under suspicion, particularly after Bennett sponsored petition drives in defense of some of those who had been arrested, and when Bennett led calls for the repeal of the Comstock laws. Bennett was also involved in a famous case that involved a satirical pamphlet called *"Cupid's Yokes,"* which promoted "Free Love," (and poked caustic fun of Comstock), and which Bennett helped to distribute. In 1879 in a sting operation, using trumped up charges against Bennett, Comstock managed to get Bennett arrested, claiming that he was sending "obscene tracts" through the mail.

Bennett was tried, and convicted under the Comstock Laws. He was sentenced to thirteen months hard labor, and was imprisoned, first in New York City at the infamous Ludlow Street Jail, and later at the Albany Penitentiary. While her husband was in prison, Mary Wicks Bennett took over as the publisher and editor of *"The Truth Seeker"* (her name appeared on the masthead) [6] and this small woman--an ex-Shaker with strong moral convictions of her own-- helped mount a very big and brave campaign to obtain a presidential

THE TRUTH SEEKER

A Journal of Freethought and Reform

Vol. 24. No. 12. {PUBLISHED WEEKLY.} New York, Saturday, March 20, 1897. {28 LAFAYETTE PL.} $3.00 Per Year.

FREETHINKERS OF THE PAST AND PRESENT.

D. M. BENNETT.

During the period between 1873 and 1882, D. M. Bennett exerted a greater influence in popularizing Freethought than any other man has done. Men of greater personality have enjoyed a wider circle of admirers; their writings have had a larger sale, and they have been better known to the world; but none ever accomplished so much in so short a time. He was born on a farm in the township of Springfield, Otsego county, N. Y., Dec. 23, 1818. At the age of twelve years he weighed but fifty pounds, and his frame was never powerful. He had four years of schooling at Cooperstown, N. Y.; he worked in a printing-office and in a wool-carding establishment. His ambition was to be a doctor, but his immaturity was against him. At the age of fifteen he joined the Shaker community at New Lebanon. Here he rose to the head of the medical department, and in 1845 was physician to the society. On October 79, 1846, he married the demure little Shakeress, Mary Wicks, having a few weeks previously quitted the celibate community.

Mr. Bennett got employment in a drugstore in St. Louis; afterward he embarked in the drug business for himself and made money. In 1855-7 we find him in the nursery line in Rochester; later a travelling salesman and collector for a seed firm. In 1859 he began the manufacture of proprietary medicines at Cincinnati, and in a few years became wealthy. Selling out his establishment, he invested the proceeds in various ventures, but not successfully. In 1863 and '66 he lost $30,000. Another drug store which he established at Kansas City, Mo., in 1868 was abandoned on account of dull trade. He became a brick manufacturer on Long Island; dropped that to go on the road again as a commercial traveler; landed finally at Paris, Ill., as a druggist, and thence emerged as a partner in a seed firm. Having sunk his

varied experiences found time to devote to reading, he had become a Freethinker, and a discussion with clerical opponents through the local papers published at Paris, when he was not accorded fair play by one of the editors, determined him to "start a paper of his own in which he could say anything he pleased." Hence The Truth Seeker. As an editor Bennett proved a success. He lacked a journalistic education, and he was not a word-carpenter, but he had a good command of language and was perfectly sincere in all he wrote. His writings did not cover the widest field of discussion, but by persistency and by iteration and reiteration he produced a greater impression than he could ever have done by scattering his blows or attempting to expound the universe. He was too much in earnest to attempt writing in the lighter vein, and he was unconscious of the humor that some of his writings contain. His style was a trifle quaint, but it was effective. Bennett did not belong to the school of "higher critics." The plain facts were quite satisfactory to him, and he preferred them stated in English. He was much like Paine in this respect, and if charged with harshness he might have replied with Paine that compassion toward error is an insult to truth. As a writer he was not only able but prolific. Somebody once advised him to read more and write less, but he answered that when the truths he was expounding had become accepted it would be time to look up some new ones. A glance at his published books shows that his industry was remarkable. His literary and journalistic career covered only the period between 1873 and 1882. One year of this time was spent in confinement, one year on a voyage around the world, and one season in Europe. Nevertheless he found time to write "The World's Sages, Think-

ers, and Reformers," a volume of 1,100 pages; "The Champions of the Church," a still larger work; "The Gods and Religions of Ancient and Modern Times," two volumes of a thousand pages each; "An Infidel Abroad," eight hundred pages; "A Truth Seeker Around the World," four volumes of about 750 pages each; the Humphrey-Bennett Discussion; the Bennett-Teed Discussion, besides other discussions and unnumbered columns of editorial matter and articles for The Truth Seeker. Adding to this labor be attended to the management of his paper and business, which he did so well that although he began without capital, the settlement of his estate left his widow in more than comfortable circumstances. The books he wrote and published cover almost the whole range of Freethought literature. The tree which he planted has not failed to increase and bear fruit, and the Truth Seeker Company's catalogue of Freethought and scientific works includes a thousand titles. He died near the close of his sixty-fourth year, Dec. 6, 1882.

[courtesy of Rod Bradford]

pardon from Rutherford B. Hayes for her husband. Mary's efforts resulted in a petition drive that gained thousands of signatures, as well as hundreds of letters and public statements of support. [7] People were outraged by the shabby treatment Bennett received. Among the most touching and eloquent statements of support were those that flowed from the pen of the noted Shaker Elder, Frederick Evans. Evans, who was an intellectual leader among the Believers, mounted a spirited defense of Bennett and others who were persecuted under the Comstock Laws.

Frederick Evans was a fascinating person, both as an individual and as a Shaker. He was a vegetarian, a writer, a deeply spiritual man, and a missionary who traveled widely to share the Shaker message. In 1888 Evans wrote his autobiography, which described not only his own life story, but also included lengthy passages dedicated to the Believers' intense--and in some ways odd--interpretation of Christ's/Mother Ann's Gospel. Evans emerged as a strong and liberal leader of the Shakers. As a young man, he had been influenced by his older brother George Evans, who helped found the radical Land-Reform movement. In Frederick's words "George started the Land-Reform movement in this country, on the basis of the principle laid down by Jefferson that 'the land belongs to man *in usufruct* only." (This is a reference to old Roman law, the notion that you can use someone else's land as long as you don't harm it). [8] The movement George Evans championed was remarkably radical and progressive, and was promoted by his friend the publisher Horace Greeley. The land reform movement actually led to the passage of The Homestead Act in 1862.

Frederick clearly shared many of his brother's radical views, and in their younger years the two men co-published several journals: *The Working Man's Advocate, The Daily Sentinel, and Young America*. Some of the demands of the land-reform movement included:

First: The right of man to the soil: "Vote yourself a farm."
Second: Down with monopolies, especially the United States Bank.
Third: Freedom of the public lands.
Fourth: Homesteads made inalienable....
Ninth: Equal rights for women with men in all respects
Tenth: Abolition of chattel slavery and of wages slavery. [9]

According to Evans, "This Spartan band [of reformists] was few in numbers, but there were deep thinkers among them; and all were earnest, practical workers in behalf of the downtrodden masses of humanity." [10] These progressives also firmly supported the separation of state and religion.

It is easy to understand why someone whose identity was based upon such principles would speak out loudly in support of Bennett, when DM was hounded and prosecuted by what amounted to the Thought Police:

"To the Editor of the *Tribune:*
Why do you great and powerful editors allow the God in the Constitution party to persecute unopposed D.M. Bennett, editor of the *"Truth Seeker?"* Are there any people more anxious to protect the youth of our nation from the corrupting influence of obscene publications than the Shakers? Yet, as my soul liveth, I would rather have the repeal of all the laws of suppression of vile publications than this robbing of the United States mail, these pious, lying decoy letters**, this interference with, and suppression of, free opinion on theological matters, where the orthodox infidel is just as good a man or woman as the orthodox Christian, as human liberty in his custody. What pranks before high heaven are those being played in the name of religion, when men who are like Jefferson, Franklin, and Paine--founders of our government--are being persecuted by officers of the Government which the founders gave their lives to establish. F.W. Evans Mount Lebanon, December 27,1877" [11]

**[a reference to the sting operation Comstock used to ensnare Bennett]

Evans certainly set down his views firmly; however in spite of the public outcry, Mary was not able to obtain the pardon she and thousands of others felt Derobigne deserved. She even made a personal appeal to President Hayes; and she was supported in her cause by the powerful Free Thought speaker and writer Robert Ingersoll, who went so far as to have several meetings with the President. But Hayes was unmoved and refused to intervene in the case. Bennett was forced to serve out the full term of his sentence. During his spell in the Albany County Penitentiary his health suffered, but his spirits were no doubt buoyed by visits from his old Shaker friends in New Lebanon. Bennett continued to be heard, even from the inside of his cell: he wrote scathing criticisms of conditions in the prison, and his celebrity--not to mention sales of his journal--continued to grow.

All the drama and publicity surrounding *"The Truth Seeker"* carried Mary and DM far away from their roots as Shakers, and yet the couple continued to model many principles of the Society, and in turn, many of their Shaker Brethren and Sisters remained lifelong friends. The elopement all those years ago had been a huge scandal, and had cost the Shakers dearly--in terms of lost talent--but Mary and her husband Derobigne, along with Letsey Ann Bennett and John Allen, went into the world as strong, kind, and capable people, thanks to the valuable upbringing they received at Mount Lebanon.

Part Three: Angeline

Angeline was a toddler when her family moved to Watervliet in October 1824. Probably during the winter that followed, Polly continued to nurse this youngest child; however as mentioned in an earlier chapter, there is a paucity of evidence concerning how long mothers of infants were allowed to keep their babies. By the time she was two or a bit older, little Angeline would have been moved into what amounted to the Nursery, to be raised in a communal setting with the other young girls, under the watchful eye of the Sister(s) in charge.

Angeline settled in quietly and was a good, and compliant Shaker. She quite literally leaves no early traces, other than her very neat hand, when she signed the South Family Covenant on the 28th of May, 1845. The youngest Wicks was barely 21 years old at the time. As evidenced by her impeccable script, Angeline was well educated: she had a good command of basic math, reading and geography. In addition, her domestic skills would have been prodigious: any respectable Shaker Sister of this period would have been able to cook, bake, weave, sew, embroider, knit, put up food of all kinds, make soap, produce candles, scour pots, empty stoves, do laundry, sweep and polish floors, paint windows and doors, weed the kitchen garden, collect and sort eggs, pick and process apples, beans, berries and umpteen other vegetables and fruits, change bed linens, mend shirts and cloaks, dust walls and furniture, and...in her spare time, read the newspaper.

Like all properly raised Shakers, Angeline was used to hard work, and was good at what she did. However, of her thoughts and feelings, we know nothing. As she was growing up, did she steal moments with her brothers Braman and Loren now and then? Angeline was 18--an impressionable age--when Braman moved from Watervliet to New Lebanon in the fall of 1842. Did he seek out his sister to say goodbye when he departed? Did they write letters to one another?

The following year, in August, Angeline traveled to New Lebanon in the company of Elder Brother Joseph Hodgson and Eldress Sister Hannah Wells: had she asked to go on the journey so she could visit with her brother Braman? The Watervliet group stayed for two days, and then returned home, bringing with them Sarah Bates (Issachar's daughter), who was slated to take over the Watervliet school for a spell. [1. I.N.Y.]

For Angeline, this adventure into the broader world must have been both educational and exciting. Did she come back and report to Loren on her visit to New Lebanon? The odds are that Angeline did not have many encounters with her much older brother--they resided in different Families-- but there is no doubt that the Wicks siblings communicated on a regular basis over the course of many years. It is also clear that the Prentiss clan--Polly's various siblings and cousins--played a part in Angeline's life. Several Prentiss Believers--most especially Oliver Prentiss, but also Shubel, Sylvester, Channing and Ephraim--make frequent appearances in the journals.

By the 1850s, Angeline found herself alone. Although she was surrounded by Shaker Sisters and Brethren, her own nuclear family was dwindling, and she must have felt the losses keenly. Braman had moved to New Lebanon in 1842, and a few years later he had left the Shakers and headed south to Mary and DeRobigne's home, where he died in 1849. In January 1853 Loren had eloped with Arabella. The departure of Loren meant the loss of yet another sibling: Olive, Cynthia, Lois had long since passed away, as well as Thomas, William and Braman. Angeline may have had occasional encounters with her mother Polly or her sister Nancy, but Nancy was preoccupied with her responsibilities as Deaconess/Eldress: she was much older than Angeline, and she must have been a busy and somewhat distant figure. Angeline's relationship to her mother Polly remains in the shadows, but in any case Polly and Nancy lived in the West Family at this time, and Angeline was apparently living in the South Family.

As she reached middle age, Angeline may have felt lonely and restless. She seems to have begun questioning her place among the Shakers. She kept mum however, carrying on as usual, always a productive and well behaved member of the community. On January 17, 1854, *"Angeline and Hester went to the C.F. to sew bonnets on their sewing machines."* In March of that year *"A most terrible wind...did much damage-*

-blew down some chimneys, some tin from CF barn, roof off new NF shop and much fence." [2]

There was a storm of a different kind churning in Angeline, for sometime in 1854 she made up her mind to depart from her Shaker community, the home that had nurtured her from infancy. On the 30th of January 1855--almost exactly two years after her brother had eloped with Arabella-- "Angeline Wicks turned off and Shubel went with her to Loren in New Jersey." [3] Shubel was Angeline's uncle, and he may in fact have taken Angeline to her brother Loren, but if so, the visit was a brief one, because by that summer (1855) Angeline showed up as a boarder in a humble house in Hoosick, to the northeast of Watervliet, in Rensselaer County.

According to the June 1855 census record, "AJ Wicks" had been living there "3/12" of the last year, in other words, for three months. Her relative Oliver Prentiss was also residing in the same house--owned by a woman, "S.M Rogers." [4] Oliver Prentiss was quite a character, who had been a strong presence among the Watervliet Shakers for many years, where he served in various leadership positions. "OP" often stirred up trouble of one kind or another when he suffered spiritual (and possibly other) crises. Mental illness may have run in the Prentiss family; a sister Angeline (Polly Wicks probably named her youngest baby daughter after this relative) seems to have been unstable, for she died in her twenties. Her sad passing is mentioned in Rufus Bishop's journal. March 7, 1839 brought "spring like weather" and a death: *"Angeline Prentis. Deceas'd by insanity."* The manner in which this Angeline died is not revealed; did she commit suicide? The Shakers were burdened with the care of unstable individuals quite often; the journals describe vivid dramas associated with mentally ill people, who occasionally committed violent acts against themselves and others, and had to be forcibly restrained. The Society experienced the loss of some members who took their own lives in terrible suicides.

*[March 1838] 29 We this morning learned that **Elizabeth Hanford**, at the Second family, **Hung herself** last evening, in an apple tree, close by their woodhouse. She was missing in time of the evening meeting, and search was made but she was not found until about 11 o'clock. -------Our neighbors were informed and a jury chosen to look into the matter. They bro't in Suicide by insanity.--Dr. Wright in particular was very favorable and no disagreeable reflections were cast on the believers. It was so evident that it was her own deliberate act, that not even was the body examined at all; but she was buried with the same clothes on, a winding sheet being put over.---She was buried today AM. The brethren principally attended and she was buried by the side of Morrell Baker.---*

There was one circumstance favorable to believers, tending to reflect the whole blame upon herself--viz. that she was known to have attempted to hang herself before she came among our society & her grandmother cut the rope & saved her life---she is said too, to have been led to do the like once at the North house, while she lived there. The cause which led her to this deed, perhaps can never be known by any natural or ordinary means.---- [5. I.N.Y.]

It is probably true that the Shakers lived with disproportionally high numbers of mentally unstable people in their communities. The outside world made no provision for the poor souls who suffered from depression, bi-polar disorder, or "the fits." And although the Shakers often resorted to primitive measures--locking people up, and/or restraining them roughly--they tried their best to be kind to those who suffered mental disorders.

Angeline's uncle Oliver Prentiss was an emotional man, but clearly not as unhappy or unstable as his poor sister, or the wretched Elizabeth Hanford. Over the course of many years Oliver struggled with his faith, and on occasion experienced wild moods and outbursts. Early in 1855 he finally made up his mind to leave the Watervliet community.

January 25, 1855: "OLIVER PRENTISS concluded to leave the Society --as he did not conform to the rules and orders and did a great deal of hurt. Ministry and Elders did all they could to have him do one thing or the other. Justice settled with him and took him to Troy. He talks of setting up a Society with more liberal views, etc. he appeared to feel very bad shed many tears when too late" [6 P.A.B.]

It is interesting that Oliver left the Watervliet community just five days before Angeline's departure; and he moved into the boarding house in Hoosick one month before Angeline arrived there. Possibly Oliver was in touch with Garret and Delia Van Hoosen, who lived nearby, and for whom Parmelia Wicks had by now been working as a housekeeper and companion for more than a dozen years.

The Van Hoosens were a very interesting couple who owned an impressive wood framed house in the neighborhood. [7]. Years earlier they had resided with the Watervliet Shakers, where they caused a bit of a commotion. Late in 1834 and early 1835, Garret and Delia--who had been committed Believers for some time--began to contemplate going back into the World. Rufus Bishop described how the matter unfolded over a period of weeks:

Nov. 20th: E[lder]. Calvin come to open his trouble about Garret Van Hoosen who it seems has imbibed a sense in opposition to the Order of believers... After dinner I went & held a long talk with Garret, and labored to convince him ...[to stay]

Nov. 22nd Brother Issachar came to our shop before breakfast & informed that Garret had hired a house in Albany, but had recanted- said he could not go away unless they carried him off- soon after breakfast Br Issachar came again & informed that he had changed his mind & was bent on going off. Shortly after that E. Calvin brought us word that he had changed again, & could not go!! and what the poor double minded man will finally do is hard to tell.

The waffling continued until February, when the Van Hoosens at last decided to leave.

Thurs. 12 Br. Issachar informed us this morning that Garret V. Hosen [sic] has again made up his mind to withdraw from our communion. In the evening we attend a meeting with the older part of the brethren, & warned them to set a godly example before the young.

Frid. 13 High wind & some snow to day. Garret & Delia went to the world yesterday. In the evening we had a meeting with the young brethren & warned them against setting bad examples before the children & other orders &c. &c.

Tues. 17 Snowed nearly all day- Garret Van Hosen[sic], with Delia, his mother, father in law & others came with 4 waggons [sic] after their movable property. [8. R.B.]

Four wagon-loads of property represented a lot of goods; Garrett and Delia came from comfortable circumstances and went back into the world quite capable of fending for themselves, and perhaps with a new appreciation of social justice after their stint with the Believers. Garret Van Hoosen soon emerged as a leader in the abolitionist movement--he served as the local president of the Liberty Party-- and there is strong evidence that the Van Hoosen home in Hoosick Falls was a stop on the Underground Railroad. [9] Although Garret and Delia remained childless all their lives, they took in others in need, including Parmelia Wicks, who lived with them for many years as their housekeeper and friend. Upon his death in the spring of 1857, Garret did "Give and bequeath unto our trusty and well beloved Miss Parmelia Wicks...five hundred dollars." [10]

Like the Van Hoosens, Parmelia Wicks had earlier lived with the WV Shakers. She had been brought to the community by her mother Lydia, along with her brother and sister in the mid-1820s. Lydia Wicks came and went from the Shakers more than once, but eventually she and her children Noah and Eliza departed for good. Parmelia remained with the Shakers, and went on to sign the Covenant. She doesn't appear in any record until early in 1837, when she was blamed for an outbreak of restlessness among some of the young people. Accused of being "a ring-leader of disorder & rebellion" among the girls, Parmelia was "removed" on January 17, 1837. With hindsight, Parmelia was probably no more or less guilty of fomenting rebellion than others, for it was only a matter of months before several young Sisters in the South Family began experiencing visions, and by late summer 1837 a full- scale revival commenced, as the "Era of Manifestations" erupted and took powerful hold of the entire community.

Parmelia meanwhile moved back to Schaghticoke to be with her mother Lydia Wicks, where she soon --like her mother-- joined the Presbyterian Church [11]. By the middle of the next decade she had moved to Hoosick, and taken up residence as housekeeper and companion to Garret and Delia Van Hoosen. Parmelia never married, and she was able to accumulate considerable wealth: her will lists many items that would have been far beyond the reach of the average household servant of the time. [12]

It is likely that Angeline was in touch with Parmelia-- perhaps this Wicks cousin sent advice about securing a job as a housekeeper. There can be no question that given her degree of literacy, not to mention her training in the "domestic arts," Angeline would have been an ideal candidate for such a position. Not long after she departed from her Shaker family, Angeline seems to have found employment as a housekeeper for one John M. Percey, a farmer and widower with four children, whose house was very near the place where Angeline first boarded when she came to Hoosick Falls (the Percey home was also not far from the Van Hoosen's).

The 1860 census indicates that Angeline was "married within the last year" to Percey, a much older man. In marrying this widower with four growing children, Angeline took on a lot of responsibility, and it wasn't long before she had a child of her own: in January 1865, she gave birth to a son. She named the little boy William Loren Percey-- perhaps Angeline named her newborn after William Wicks, the brother who had perished so far away and long ago on the banks of the Rio Grande. Her husband John Percey also had a brother named William, so the name seemed fitting. The baby's middle name, Loren, was a tribute to Angeline's one remaining, beloved brother.

Angeline kept active during these years, tending to her new baby, as well as caring for her older step-children; there was scant time to read a newspaper or compose a letter. However, somehow this busy mother *made* time to keep in touch with those she loved, for by the time of the *next* census, in 1870, Angeline's sister Mary Wicks Bennett was living with the Percey family, and working nearby as a "domestic." [13] During this period Mary and Derobigne were experiencing financial difficulties, so it made sense for Angeline to help her sister through a rough patch. This is yet another example of how the Wicks siblings reached out over long distances to care for one another.

Soon enough, it was Angeline's turn to face hardship straight on: her husband died on December 15, 1874. Willie was not quite ten when his father passed away, but the other Percey children were all much older by this time--the next youngest son (named John after his father) was 18, and the rest were adults. John M. Percey died intestate; a younger brother, Elon Percey, was appointed to "administer and faithfully dispose of all and singular goods and chattel and credits of the said deceased." [14] Without the guaranteed security of a home and necessary cash, Angeline was left out in the cold, almost literally; soon after her husband's death, Angeline and her son William moved to New Jersey to live with Loren, who by this time had amassed quite a lot of money and was a well established businessman.

Angeline and William settled in for some years with Loren in Beverly, Burlington County, New Jersey. Willie attended school there, and learned about the business world from his uncle. Within a few years, as often happens, William met his future wife in high school: he fell in love with Helen Wilson. Willie and Helen were almost exactly the same age, both bright and able students. They married in their early twenties, and their first daughter was born in November 1887. Soon after that, the young couple moved west, where they settled in Pasadena, California and where William began a career as a book-keeper. By the late 1890s, William Loren Percey and Helen had three daughters, and they had achieved a comfortable lifestyle: their household included a 15 year old servant named Helena, the daughter of German immigrants. [15]

Whether Angeline stayed with Loren in New Jersey after her son and daughter-in-law moved west is not clear. Loren died in 1893, and around this time--probably soon after Loren's death-- Angeline moved to California, to be closer to her grand-children. Angeline Wicks Percey died at the age of 72 in Pasadena on January 24, 1896, faraway from upstate New York. However in an unusual act, her body was brought back east for burial in the Hoosick Rural Cemetery. Angeline's remains lie close to her husband and his first wife Patience. Their single stone states that Angeline M. Percey was "the wife of John M. Percey." The first wife, Patience, had passed away at aged 42 (she may have died in childbirth); John was 62 when he died; Angeline lived to be 72 years, well into old age by the standards of the day.

In the mid to late 1800s Hoosick was a thriving place, blessed with excellent water power, fertile land, and several small manufacturing enterprises. Entrepreneurs made a good living in Hoosick and Hoosick Falls, and a number of churches and community organizations sprang up in this bustling area not far from the Vermont border. Sadly, today Hoosick is a worn down town, its buildings crumbling, its surviving residents facing a scandal involving contaminated water. The cemetery where Angeline Wicks Percey rests is showing signs of neglect. The good times are long gone.

Part Four: Loren, the Linchpin

When Loren and Arabella rushed off to be married back in January 1853, some passionate scenes must have ensued, once the couple shed their Shaker garments, donned new fashionable suits, and "presented themselves at the Hymenial altar and were made one flesh." How sweet their romance must have been, full of tenderness and discovery. One wonders what mode of transport the couple took to Kentucky, and how long the journey was? One way or another, within a few days they arrived at the home of Loren's sister Mary and Derobigne.

After the rocky start in Kentucky, DM had opened a drug store--interestingly, using money from a small inheritance left by a deceased brother of Mary's [1]. This brother was likely to have been Braman, who had passed away at the Bennett home in 1848. Although Bennett's drug store fared reasonably well, DM--as already mentioned-- was otherwise inept when it came to money matters, and by the time Loren and Arabella arrived on their honeymoon, early in 1853, Bennett was probably experiencing financial difficulties.

No doubt Loren and Derobigne talked about the challenges facing ex-Shakers as they moved out into the world. It is interesting to contemplate their conversations, when these very different men--one tall and perhaps laconic, the other short and gregarious--sat down together and discussed the vicissitudes and practical dilemmas they now faced. It is possible the two men agreed to collaborate on a joint venture; what is known is that by the mid-1850s both men had dealings in the mid-west.

When Loren departed from his life-long home with the Shakers he was presented with a few valued tools and a little money; it was customary for the Trustees to provide a small "starter kit" for those going into the world. On his arm was his beautiful young bride, but otherwise Loren possessed little else but his wits. In this respect, he was in command of a huge knowledge base (as we would say nowadays) of practical skills. In no time Loren proved himself an inventor, and he started filing patents. As a rule, Shakers did *not* file patents, although they are given credit for a number of useful inventions, including the circular saw and the flat broom. Freegift Wells was said to have been the man behind the circular saw, which was in operation by around 1817. Wells himself wrote: "The Shakers consider the discovery too useful to be monopolized by a patent, and consented to my giving it publicity as public property." [2] Occasionally Shaker Brethren were involved in legal matters concerning machinery: in October 1843, *"Henry Bennett taken to Albany via R.R.--for an evidence in a law case, about a plaining machine--two parties are in strife about the Patent."* [3 I.N.Y.] In this instance, the Shaker Brother was presumably merely acting as a witness; however Henry Bennett may well have conversed with his nephew DM regarding legal matters and patents, and it is quite possible DM passed along the gist of some of these conversations to Loren.

No law said Loren couldn't make gains from his own knowledge base. During the 1850s, Loren and Arabella seem to have hit the road--rolling restless souls--and explored various life options in various locations. Along the way, Loren left a trail of patents. [4] On Sept. 9, 1854, Loren J. Wicks, of New York, New York, filed patent number 11,708 for " *A Method of Operating Guide-Rollers and Feed-Clamps in Sawing Machines."* In 1855 L. J. Wicks filed a patent for a special straw-cutter in Paterson, New Jersey. In 1859 he filed two patents in Racine, Wisconsin for " Churns." Back in New York, on January 31, 1860, Loren J. Wicks shares the news, in Patent number 27,015 that he had "invented certain new and useful Improvements in Skates." He goes on, somewhat later, to file a patent for a special design for bottles. This patent is dated February 1, 1870. Loren had settled in southwestern New Jersey by this time, where he was running a success-ful fruit canning business. Loren seems to have hit his stride with the bottle patent.

Sadly, along the road to success, tragedy entered Loren's life, for by the time he filed the bottle patent, Loren was a widower. Like so many Shaker sisters, Arabella was infected with tuberculosis. Whether she and Loren ever conceived a child is not known (there is no evidence Arabella ever gave birth), but the poor young woman must have been ill for some time, coughing and wheezing her way along the roads and in rented rooms, as she and Loren moved from place to place. Loren himself no doubt also had tuberculosis-- the journals tell of him spending time in the sick house, suffering from "the lung fever. " But Loren was more fortunate than his

[Photo: Nora Ritchie]

young wife--perhaps because of all the time he spent out-doors--and he never succumbed to the disease. Arabella's death notice appeared in the New York Daily Tribune on Friday September 6, 1860, under WICKS: ---"*On Thursday after-noon, September 6, of inflammation of the lungs, Mrs. Arabella M., wife of Loren J. Wicks, aged 25 years, 5 months, 12 days. The relatives and friends of the family are invited to attend the funeral from their late residence, No. 307 Gold Street, Brook-lyn, without further notice, at 11 o'clock a.m. on Saturday.*" [5] Arabella's grave can still be seen today, in Lot 13341, Section 18, of the famous Green-Wood Cemetery in Brooklyn.

The joy Loren and Arabella shared as newly-weds had been short-lived. Whether the Wicks ever returned to Watervliet as a couple is not known; whether the news of Arabella's death traveled back to her Shaker family is not known. Perhaps the Shaker Brethren and Sisters had Loren and his poor wife in their hearts when they sang a new song, one which first appeared in Watervliet around 1860, and whose sweet tune and words certainly resonate: "*Now my dear compan-ions, is the time to start anew, A-new, a-new, for the kingdom of Heaven...With faith and zeal and courage strong, we will ever be marching on, Toiling on, struggling on, for a perfect Heaven.*" [6]

After Arabella's death in 1860, Loren had to carry on alone; he seems to have had both the emotional strength and practical intelligence needed to face the future with resolve. Perhaps no other Wicks family member was as industrious as Loren. Mary-- by way of her husband's reputation-- may have gained more "fame," but it was Loren who succeeded in business, and it was Loren who "held it all together." He was the linchpin.

His fruit canning business brought in a comfortable income, which afforded him a good home and extra savings, as well as the luxury of being able to describe himself on the Beverly, New Jersey 1880 census form as "retired." Loren was

66 years old, and by this time then 57-year-old Angeline was "keeping house" (the census phrase) for her brother, and Willie was growing up in a home with two good role models. It must have been comforting for brother and sister to be once more together as a family, and to have a young person in the house.

It was Loren the successful fruit canner who had the means to purchase a substantial burial plot in the Green-Wood cemetery in Brooklyn, where an imposing obelisk still stands in tribute to Arabella. In addition, the Wicks family plot contains a huge and impressive memorial to none other than Derobigne Mortimer Bennett, Loren's brother-in-law. DM Bennett passed away in December 1882, and a few months later Loren purchased an addendum to his plot, which he conveyed to his sister Mary Wicks Bennett. On June 7, 1883 the brother and sister conveyed the now expanded Wicks family plot over to the Green-Wood Cemetery. [7]

By this point a commotion was brewing concerning DeRobigne Bennett's burial in Green-Wood, which was of course a Christian cemetery. What rights did this "infidel" have, to secure a resting place among the angels? The public debate was heated, but in the end enough powerful people gave their blessings for the project to proceed. The towering memorial stone, with a lengthy tribute to D.M. Bennett, was finally dedicated on June 13, 1884. [8] The year after her husband's death, Mary sold the *Truth Seeker* and she then settled down to live a quiet life until her death at age 79, in July 1898. She apparently often felt DM's presence nearby [9] Mary's remains lie next to her husband in the Wicks plot. Loren himself was put to rest in the ground at Green-Wood a few years before his sister, on May 11, 1893. (He died on May 9, 1893 in New Jersey). Loren lived to be just short of 79 years, the same age his sister Mary was when she died. Sadly, there is no marker over Loren's grave. This is a puzzle, since there *is* a carved stone over Mary's resting place. Mary out-lived her brother: why did she not arrange for a stone to honor her brother? By this time the Wicks plot was owned by Green-Wood Cemetery: perhaps the cost and paperwork were prohibitive for the lonely widow.

In any case Loren Wicks certainly deserves thanks for all the ways in which he stood by his family and friends, not to mention, for the practical application of his many inventions. It is sad that there exists no epitaph for Loren. Perhaps we can compose our own thanks, tweaking a Shaker song to pay fitting tribute to Loren J. Wicks, the man who contributed so much to his Shaker Brethren and Sisters, and then went out into the world to do more good works as a businessman and family man:

"O-Ho the pretty chain, that binds us all together...O-Ho its links are love, that's wrought by faithful labor...And while this love we do maintain, our spirits flow together, Within this chain we will remain, forever close in Loren's warm embrace." [10]

The impressive Memorial erected to the memory of Derobigne Bennett is on the left. Mary and Derobigne lie together, and to the right Arabella rests near the obelisk. Loren Wicks is also buried here, but sadly this ex-Shaker who did so much for his own family and others, has no head stone. [Photo: Nora Ritchie]

CHAPTER SEVEN

The Last Shakers**

It is interesting but not surprising that of all the Wicks, the two who remained life-long Believers were Polly--the mother of ten children-- and Nancy, her first-born daughter. When this large family showed up at the Great Gate at Watervliet, back in October 1824, Polly was 38-years-old and Nancy had just turned 17. Both women must have been exhausted from the long journey, with crying and hungry children in tow, and bulky luggage to manage. Imagine what the tired family beheld when they were ushered into the South Family quarters, where all was quiet, the tables were neatly set for the evening meal, and properly made beds awaited them upstairs in the dwelling house. That night, with little Angeline snuggling by her side, Polly must have drifted into her first deep sleep in many days.

As for Nancy, all her life she had been a big sister, helping her mother cope with the younger ones: so many little bottoms to clean, scraped knees to rinse, and always hands reaching up, "Hold me, hold me!" Upon arriving in the Watervliet community--as if by some miracle-- all those little dependent children found other arms to hold them. Seventeen-year-old Nancy woke up to an utterly fresh world, one where she was invited to "open her mind" and become a whole new person.

**This chapter title refers to the last of the WICKS family who were Shakers; as of this writing two remaining Believers carry on the faith at the United Society (of Shakers) in Sabbathday Lake, Maine.

Within a very short time this strong and capable teenager took to her new role as "Sister Nancy," and thrived.

By 1830 both mother Polly and Nancy were still living in the South Family. Three of the Wicks girls--Olive, Cynthia and Lois-- were severely compromised with tuberculosis by now, but it is unlikely that either Polly or Nancy spent much if any time nursing their natural family members, since they were living some distance away. But mother and daughter would no doubt have grieved together at Olive's funeral in June of 1831, and over Cynthia's grave later that year, and once again the following spring, when they gathered in April 1832 to bid farewell to Lois. Polly lost three children in less than a year; one envisions her picking sweet fresh violets to place on Lois's grave, and accepting a kind embrace from her Sister friends. Funerals were occasions for the larger community to come together, to sing and to celebrate the life of the dear departed one, now released into the care of the angels.

• • •

Sister Nancy no doubt made friends easily, and was an extremely competent young woman. By the early 1830s she had signed the Covenant and was emerging as a leader in the community; and within less than ten years of her arrival at Watervliet, Nancy Wicks was serving as Deaconess in the South Family, a position of substance and responsibility--bearing in mind that a typical Shaker family comprised approximately 70-100 people. The South Family Covenant/ Constitution from 1831 clearly defines these roles:

"The Deacons and Deaconesses of families are entrusted with the care and oversight of the domestic concerns of their respective families. It is their duty to maintain good order; to watch over, counsel, and direct the members in their various occupations, as occasion may vary or require; to make application to the officer Deacons or Trustees for whatever supplies are needed in the several

departments of the family; to maintain union, harmony and good understanding with the said office Deacons; and to report to their Elders the state of matters which fall under their recognition & observation." [1]

Deacons and Deaconesses were very much in charge of day-to-day matters, but bore no responsibility for the "bigger" interests of the Shaker community, especially where commerce and communication with the World's People were involved. Sister Nancy served for some time before asking to be relieved of her position in late 1835: *"Nancy Wicks is released from her lot of care as deaconess and Eliza Ask takes her place."* [2] For the better part of the next decade, Nancy served on-and-off in various senior positions in both the South and the West families. It is clear from the records that these jobs were often rotated around among the most responsible and capable members of the community. Managing the affairs of such a large number of people was challenging even on a *good* day; when sickness and personality clashes flared up, the challenges must have been considerable. In addition, the South Family served as the "Welcome Wagon" at Watervliet, and-- as previously mentioned--at various times this group was besieged with large numbers of wanderers seeking food and shelter.

The following journal entries mention Nancy, and reveal how stressful the senior jobs must have been:

7 May 1837 "Ann Bowser, second Eldress, on account of ill health is released from the eldership and Eliza Ask takes her place. Eliza Ask being released from her lot as deaconess, Nancy Wicks takes her place."

Oct. 24, 1844 "Elmira Watkins is released from her lot as Second Eldress, by her own request, on account of ill health, and takes her former lot as First Deaconess. And Nancy Wicks takes her place."

Jan. 27, 1845 "Nancy Wicks is released from her lot as Second Eldress, by her own request, and takes her former lot with Elmira a Second Deaconess. And Maryann Ayers takes her place." [3]

In June 1845, Nancy enjoyed the diversion of a major trip, along with two other senior members of the Watervliet Society: *E. Issachar, Eld[resses] Rebekah & Nancy Wicks Started this morning on a long Journey in the West, to search after hungry souls. It is expected that they will visit Groveland before they return.* [4 R.B.] It is not clear how long they were away, or how many souls they converted.

On May 29 1849, the record states that *"Elmira Watkins a Covenant Member and first deaconess of the Family for many years is released and removed to the Second Family and Nancy Wicks takes her place."* [5] During this period, Nancy moved back-and-forth between the South Family and the West Family. She was a mature woman, respected for her strengths, and needed for her leadership skills. But the strain showed, as she more than once made requests to be relieved of her posts. *In November, 1849, Nancy Wicks a Covenant Member and first Deaconess of this family, is released and removed to the Second family..."* [6] Soon after Nancy was again persuaded to serve as a Deaconess and Eldress, but she was approaching fifty, and this hard working woman must have been ready for retirement.

If Nancy stood out as a leader among the Shakers, by contrast, her mother Polly lived a very quiet life. There is virtually no reference at all to Polly Wicks in the journals. There were other more prominent Polly's among the Watervliet Shakers--Polly Vedder and Polly Bates--whose activities and responsibilities were noted in various records, making for some confusion; but Polly Wicks, the tired mother of ten who settled down into peace and obscurity in 1824, rarely if ever seems to have caused a ripple of interest or concern for anyone. Sister Polly performed her chores dutifully, without any protest; and except toward the very end of her life, she never seems to have suffered from an illness or injury that was serious enough to warrant special mention. It isn't even known whether she could read or write. Like so many women who found refuge among the kind and sensible Shakers, Polly went about her business, living a long life, and dying without much fuss.

Poor Polly *did* suffer in the waning months of her life, for in June 1863: *"the Ministry all goes to the Second Family to make some arrangements concerning Polly Wicks making a journey to a foreign physician & surgeon to have a cancer extracted."* [7]

One hopes Polly didn't experience too much pain before she passed away; those last few weeks must have been hard, but no doubt Polly bore her cross with her usual quiet fortitude. Polly was 77 years old when she died on September 29, 1863. She had lived with the Shakers for almost forty years, and for all of that time--up until the very end--this quiet, unassuming woman had enjoyed a secure and comfortable life--both practically and spiritually--with her adopted Shaker Family.

Of Polly's private thoughts, over those many years, we know nothing. She signed the Covenant, and was doubtless a committed Believer. Perhaps she was shy, as the records are so quiet with respect to this woman. Was she close friends with some of the other Sisters? Did she keep in touch with her children? Did she feel a tinge of maternal pride when her daughter Nancy took on the mantle of responsibility as Deaconess and Eldress? Was Polly informed when her sons Thomas and William and Braman passed away? Was she shocked when Loren left with young Arabella? Did she raise her voice in joyful song each week at Meeting?

Polly Wicks remains an enigma. At the end of her life, having played a part in what were the best years of the remarkable Shaker experiment, Polly simply went to sleep without complaining or commenting on the scene.

Like her mother before her, Nancy was an example of how the Shaker lifestyle tended to be good for one's health, especially that of women: Nancy died on August 29, 1895, just shy of what would have been her 88th birthday. Never having run the risks associated with pregnancy, and having otherwise benefitted from nutritious food and clean living, Nancy far exceeded the life expectancy of the time. Her life had stretched all the way from the epitome of Shaker communities--in the 1820s and 30s-- to the end of the century, by which time membership was falling precipitously, as the old Sisters and Brethren passed away, and few young people joined or signed the Covenant. By this time, the closing and consolidation of Shaker communities had become a necessary but sad fact of the life.

Remarkably, of the twelve Wicks who arrived in Watervliet in 1824, nine actually committed themselves seriously to the Shaker cause. There is every indication that the three teenage daughters--Olive, Cynthia, and Lois--were on their way

A group of Shakers at the Watervliet site, in front of the Brethren's Workshop, this posed picture was taken in the mid 1890s, about the time that Sister Nancy--the last member of the Wicks family living as a Shaker-- died. The faces of these individuals would have been familiar to Nancy Wicks. [Shaker Heritage Society]

to becoming faithful Believers: the fact that Lovina Bates left her hymnal book to Olive is a touching confirmation of the girl's commitment to the Shaker Gospel. Tragically, just when they were entering what should have been their most productive years, these sweet sisters succumbed to tuberculosis, the disease that took away all too many young Shakers (especially girls) prematurely.

Of the remaining Wicks, it is amazing how many years of labor they contributed to their Shaker families. It is true that the Wicks children were listed as poor dependents back in 1825 shortly after their impoverished parents brought them to Watervliet; and it is true that in the following decade, older Sisters and Brethren took on the burden of collectively raising these children to become good community members. So yes, in the beginning, the Wicks children in effect got more than they gave. However, soon the scales tipped the other way, and adding together the years that Polly, Nancy, Loren, Mary, Braman and Angeline spent with the Shakers, the results are note-worthy. Polly lived with the Believers for all of the rest of her life, just short of forty years, from 1824 to 1863; Nancy gave *seventy* years of her life to the Shakers; Loren spent twenty-nine years of his life at Watervliet, during which time--once he reached his teenage years--he worked ceaselessly, constructing buildings, mending dams, hauling goods to market, fixing fences, leading work parties to-and-from the river farm on the Mohawk. Loren's days were full of physical exertion, and each night, this strong tall man no doubt fell into bed with tired muscles and a clear conscience.

Over in the New Lebanon community, Mary Wicks lived as a Shaker for twenty-two years, and once grown she served variously as a care-taker of the girls and as a bonnet-maker. Mary probably had a taste for wild berries, and she was unquestionably a deeply spiritual person, who played a small but significant role during the Era of Manifestations. Mary's brother Braman may have been a restless man, but he too spent over twenty-two years with the Shakers, and created some lovely furniture along the way. Lastly, quiet and compliant Angeline lived for almost thirty-one years with the Shakers before she decided to explore the world beyond the gates of home. Together, these four Wicks siblings--not counting Nancy--actually contributed over *one hundred years* of labor to their Shaker communities between 1830 and 1855.

The Wicks provided vital labor during the peak years of the Shaker drama, when this fascinating social, economic and religious experiment was thriving. But by choosing to move out into the greater society, the departing Wicks were a perfect example of how and why the Shaker world shrank during the second half of the 19th century. Before the Civil War, much of the United States' economy was agrarian-based; during the war, in the North a mighty industrial machine surged to life, when factories revved up to produce armaments and other materials. The pulsing sounds of industrialization did not slow down at the war's end, rather, hundreds of mills and factories opened up--in the South as well as the North-- just as the country's population swelled with immigrants. The result was that thousands of people found work in the new economy. The Homestead Act meanwhile freed up land on the Plains, so thousands more men and women rushed to settle the West. Once again, as had happened in the opening decades of the century, during the 1870s and 1880s restless Americans were on the move. How could young Shakers not be enticed by jobs in the newly formed factories, or by the call of the Wild West?

The leave-taking may have been bittersweet--saying good-bye to life-long Brethren and Sisters was hard on the heart-- but as the nineteenth century marched on, young people departed their Shaker communities in droves.

The accompanying lists are small samplings of what began as a "drip-drip" leak of members, and gradually expanded to become a virtual flood of departing individuals. Shaker records, over the decades, are filled with pages of names, with accompanying indications that members have returned "to the world," or that they "went away." Often the stark notation simply says "Gone." Gone, gone, gone... a bell tolling the sad, doleful truth.

[New York State Library Manuscripts and Special Collections]

The names listed here are individuals who resided in the Watervliet South Family for many years. These were so-called "Covenanted" Believers--those who had signed the Covenant and committed themselves to the Gospel. Many played leading roles in their Families, and so many--especially among the men-- abandoned the cause. "Gone, gone, gone, gone."

AFTERWARD

"If there is an industrious, temperate, frugal, virtuous,

and happy people in the world,

they are the Shakers." [1]

One of the most influential Shakers in the second half of the nineteenth century was Elder Frederick W. Evans. Elder Evans (already mentioned in a previous chapter) was both an intellectual as well as an extremely able farmer, writer, and administrator. In the late 1850s, at the North Family in New Lebanon, Evans oversaw the construction of a vast five story stone barn, which when completed housed the most advanced agricultural technology. Although badly damaged by a fire in 1972, this mighty stone barn still stands today as a testament to Evans as an individual, and to the Shakers' community-minded skills as designers and builders.*

Elder Frederick was a "think-outside-the-box" man, whose ideas and outspokenness sometimes rankled more conservative members of the Society. With membership in Shaker communities dwindling, and virtually no new prospects appearing, Evans realized there was an urgent need to take his Society's message out into the world. Through lectures and pamphlets, letters and poems, Brother Frederick spread the news, covering all sorts of topics, including "matters of diet, health, burial practices, government, farming, temperance, land ownership, women's rights, working conditions, pacifism and religious beliefs." [2] Evans reached out

---

* (As of this writing the New Lebanon barn is undergoing a multi-year major renovation).

to mainstream Protestant denominations, spoke in various other public settings, and even journeyed to England twice, seeking converts. [3]

In many ways Evans was an excellent standard bearer for the Shakers: he was a "modern man"--someone who embraced progressive causes and experimented with new practical techniques in agriculture and other areas. He nudged his fellow Believers ever forward, as he encouraged greater intercourse with the outside world. However Evans had a high opinion of himself, and tended to go on and on, often in an excessively controlling manner. According to one contemporary observer "Evans has got only one string to his instrument, and upon this he is constantly playing." [4] Elder Evans liked to hear himself talk, it seems, and his large ego no doubt irritated fellow members of the Society.

During this period in the later 1800s, there was another challenge: even while some Shaker communities were beginning to loosen their outlook, and gradually relax some of their traditional customs--dress codes were changing, individuals were on occasion allowed to keep personal tokens--the decision to join the Society and to become a *true* Believer still involved a huge leap-of-faith, and much self-sacrifice. This sacrifice included forfeiting all personal property, as well as embracing celibacy. Entering the closed world of a Shaker community still meant turning away--resolutely-- from mainstream society.

As the American economy rocketed into a new era of industrialization, the contrast between agrarian-based Shaker villages--with their aging members, aging properties, and shrinking work forces-- and the go-go bigger world couldn't have been greater. In the United States, toward the end of the nineteenth century, life's possibilities seemed limitless: more and more jobs beckoned as new industries developed, social mobility was on the rise, and the opportunity to own land out on the Plains loomed large. Once again, as had happened at the opening of the century, people everywhere were on the move, seeking adventure and ever more independence. The American Dream was in full swing.

It is no wonder that the Wicks--along with countless others who had once been secure in their Shaker villages--wanted to be part of the action. Although they didn't succeed at getting "rich quick," Derobigne and Mary played their part in this roiling drama, as they moved from state-to-state, experimenting with businesses of all kinds, meeting people from all walks of life, and eventually challenging the status quo. For his part, Loren--although he had to carry on without his pretty young bride--was able to cash in on some of his patents, and eventually set up a lucrative fruit canning business. As the surviving Wicks traveled the roads, and chugged along the newly built rail lines in search of new jobs or business opportunities, the lessons they had learned while being raised Shaker still resonated. Even after he lost his beautiful Arabella, Loren--the family linchpin--went on to provide a home for his sister Angeline and his nephew William, as well as to make possible the construction of an impressive monument to his brother-in-law and other family members in the famous Green-Wood Cemetery. From birth to death, the Wicks stayed in touch, sharing resources and love.

Perhaps it was in this matter of "family" that the Shakers were naive, and went a bit wrong: throughout the decades, the Elders and Eldresses, with help from the Deacons and Deaconesses, worked ceaselessly to offer *substitute* parents and siblings, to form *substitute* Families that would comprise a more perfect world. However this process--building what amounted to artificial families--was a constant struggle, because even those who declared themselves true Believers continued to maintain connections with their blood relatives. The records reveal a steady stream of people coming and going, often in states of high anxiety, as they dropped off children, and then returned to take them back; as they renounced feckless partners, and then sought to be reunited once again with the same weak souls. In the end, the ties that bound extended families--conventional families--together, often proved stronger than the new social units the Shakers sought to create.

The Wicks saga demonstrates both the positive impacts of Shaker life, and one of its central flaws. Over the course of more than fifty years, the Wicks remained faithful to their Shaker roots and friends, even while they chose to live, ultimately, *outside* the Shaker world, within the circle of their *own* families.

Carrying on into the next generation, it's too bad that neither Angeline nor Loren lived to see William Percey's rise. He certainly benefitted, albeit indirectly, from Shaker principles: by middle age, Angeline's son had achieved remarkable success at the Southern California Edison Company, where he held senior positions as Treasurer and eventually Vice-President. Angeline no doubt imbued in William the same qualities of discipline and hard work that she had learned in her Shaker family. Early on, William was taught to do a job *well:* whether one is folding clothes, or creating a piece of fine furniture, or weaving a fancy cloak for sale, each action must add up to a perfect product. For his part, William's Uncle Loren may have seemed the quintessence of a self-made-man, but everything he accomplished derived from his training as a Shaker. Loren likely passed on these important lessons to his nephew: "See what you can do, when you keep moving forward, with persistence and without self-pity, always seeking to make the world a better place?"

What an interesting study it would make, to track down all those who departed from the Shakers in the mid-1800s and to examine how many--like the Van Hoosens--went on to become actively involved in progressive causes such as the abolitionist movement, rights for women, and redressing the working conditions of the poor; and/or how many others succeeded as entrepreneurs in the booming economy of the times?

What of those Believers who stayed behind, like Sister Polly and Eldress Nancy? Did these two life-long Shakers ever fret over their departed family members: what of their *souls?* Mother Ann's visions of purity were transcendent, and by contrast her portrayals of the devil's temptations were vivid and frightening. It may not have been true for all who signed the Covenant--those who came-and-went in short order surely could not claim to be true Believers--but for most individuals who confessed their sins by opening their minds in the *fullest* sense, the process of embracing the Shaker faith had a profound and long-lasting effect.

Emulating Christ's--Mother Ann's--pure love through daily actions of devotion was a constant challenge for the Believers, but this dedicated lifestyle brought with it many rewards, both large and small. Those who gave themselves up to Christ felt his/her presence in the world around them-- in the little birds, in the words of hymns, in the clouds and rain, in all of the actions of daily life. Shakers experienced a world full of spirits, and for those who left the Society, it must not have been easy to leave behind the rituals associated with the faith. During their lively worship services, members were transported through song and dance, and often experienced out-of-body visions. Skeptics may claim that such "fits" were simply the result of hyperventilation or of group hysteria, but for Believers, the spirit world was close by, and very real.

Derobigne and Mary Bennett, in spite of their firm stand against the tyranny of some Bible-thumping self-righteous Christians, remained deeply committed to Spiritualism throughout their lives. Many self-proclaimed "deists" were drawn to Theosophism--which had its roots in Spiritualism- -and which flourished during the latter half of the nineteenth century and well into the twentieth (and carries on to this day through the Waldorf movement). Theosophy--combining

the Greek words "theos" meaning "God," and "sophia" meaning "wisdom," is an interesting blend of Eastern and Western
thought, which mixes religion and philosophy and empha-
sizes the fluid, eternal nature of life. Theosophists/Spiritual-
ists believe that life is ever-lasting. After her husband died,
Mary maintained that she felt his presence still nearby [5].
As the co-editor of "The Truth Seeker," Mary had journeyed
very far away, both literally and figuratively, from her Shaker
roots. Perhaps Mary's spirit still resides companionably, side-
by-side with members of her own Wicks family, as well as
with her many Shaker siblings. May the Wicks all rest in
peace and simplicity, in eternal tribute to the lovely and most
famous Shaker song:

"Tis the gift to be simple
'Tis the gift to be free
'Tis the gift to come down
where we ought to be
And when we find ourselves in the place just right
'Twill be in the valley of love and delight
When true simplicity is gained,
To bow and to bend we shan't be ashamed,
To turn, turn, will be our delight,
'Till by turning, turning we come round right."

In many respects, the Shakers *did* "come round right."
They were hard working people who strove mightily to make
a better world: one that was peaceful and that provided everyone with economic and social security. Of all the Utopian
experiments that were attempted in this country during the
1800s--from Brook Farm in Massachusetts, to New Harmony
in Indiana, to the Oneida Community in upstate New York-
-none thrived for as long, or was as successful as the Shaker
venture. More lives were affected by the Shaker experiment
than by all the other community efforts combined.

Perhaps it was because *common sense* ruled the lives of Shakers, as evidenced by some of their delightful guidelines. They aimed for perfection, yes; but along the way, they were eminently practical. Consider the following dictates:

"Boys under 15 years old are not allowed to play with guns; and the longer they let the guns alone, the better."

"The brethren and sisters are not allowed to wander away from their companions in hand labor without letting them know where they are going, that they may be found quickly if they should be wanted."

"Whoever borrows a tool must return it to the owner or to its proper place as soon as may be practicable."

"No beast belonging to the Church must be allowed to suffer with hunger; but all must be kept in their proper places, and properly attended to, according to their needs." [6]

Some of the statutes and ordinances did involve petty rules, but the guidelines for living were designed for the good of all--man as well as beast--to maintain order and consistency. For peace to reign, the members needed to contribute labor and love in a unified way. Shakers sought spiritual enlightenment "in the moment" as we say today.

The following words of wisdom appear in a "Circular Epistle," composed by the ministry at New Lebanon, and directed to the leadership in Watervliet: *"To our precious Brethren and Sisters in Zion, Greeting[s]...Three important questions should frequently occupy the thoughts & considerations for every true Believer. First: Where am I? Secondly: what are the duties of my Gospel day? Thirdly, what are the privileges of the occasion?"* [7]

Struggling for perfection was not an easy task, but in some very real ways, the Believers did draw close to finding heaven on earth. The Shakers were certainly correct when they observed that in the final measure "it is not the outside riches, but the inside ones that produce happiness."

NOTES

Numerous passages in this book are taken directly from original Shaker journals. The following scribes are quoted at length. In the interests of brevity, when using verbatim excerpts, the initials of the authors are used.

Bishop, Rufus. *A Journal of Passing Events: begun January 1st, 1830. By Rufus Bishop, in the 56th year of his age. Journal 1830-1839 May 18. [and ensuing volumes]* New York Public Library, Humanities and Social Sciences Division, Manuscripts and Archives Division, Shaker Manuscript Collection, 1780-1952. **"R.B."**

Buckingham, Phoebe Ann. *Diaries...* 26 bound volumes describing daily life at the Church Family in Watervliet, dating from 1837-1878. New York State Library, Manuscripts and Special Collections, Shaker Collection, SC20330, Boxes 5-9. **"P.A.B."**

Youngs, Isaac N. *A Domestic journal of daily occurrences kept by Isaac N. Youngs, January 1,1834-December 31, 1846.* 1 vol. ca. 400 p. New York State Library Manuscripts and Special Collections, Shaker Collection, SV20330, Box 19, folder 1. **"I.N.Y."** At the beginning of his journal, Youngs says: "**N.B. Those in the family who wish to peruse this journal, may take it from here, if they will write their names on the slate, in the case, and return it before the end of the month.----Thank you.**"

Background Notes

1. Binney, Charles James Fox. *The History and Genealogy of the Prentice, Or Prentiss Family, in New England, etc. From 1631 to 1863.* Boston, 1883. [Public domain]

Introduction

1. This article appeared in numerous newspapers around NYS in late January 1853 and early February 1853: from *"The Freeman's Journal"* in Cooperstown, to the *"Brooklyn Eagle,"* to the *"New York Times,"* it was reprinted (and slightly tweaked) by numerous editors. (I found copies

through various newspaper indexes including *fultonhistory.com*. *Pro-quest* and *New York Historic Newspapers (www.nyshn.org)*. *"The Brooklyn Eagle"* added the following introduction to its version of the article (which was a verbatim copy of the original): *"The Syracuse Journal gives the following account of a marriage between two Shakers. The man had lived thirty-eight years without ever having kissed a woman. The girl had stood seventeen years, and it is gallant to suppose, with equal abstinence. Upon the latter point, however, we are without any direct testimony."*

2. Bushman, Richard Lyman. *Joseph Smith: Rough Stone Rolling*. New York: Alfred A. Knopf, 2005. pp.19-20.

3. Ibid, frontispiece.

4. "Canal History," *www* canals.ny.gov/history/html

5. *"A Summary View of the Millennial Church, or United Society of Believers, commonly called Shakers..."* Second edition, revised and improved. Republished by the United Society, with Approbation of the Ministry. Albany: 1848. Printed by C. Van Benthuysen. Section 4, p. 2. New- York Historical Society Main Collection. BX9771 .A3

CHAPTER ONE
The Wicks Arrive at Watervliet

1. *"Memorandum of events of the Second Order, 1818-1836.* 1 v. 70 p. An anonymous journal (possibly composed by Eunice Johnson?), New York State Library Shaker Collection, SC 20330 Box 2, folder 1.

2. Mary Marshall Dyer and Eunice Chapman never forgave the Shakers for "stealing" their children from them, and both women gained considerable fame and notoriety from writing books lambasting the sect. Dyer made money on the lecture circuit, while Chapman succeeded--after a lengthy struggle--in getting the New York State Legislature to grant her the one and only "Legislative Divorce" ever passed [see Ilyon Woo in bibliography). Both women ended up bitter. The Shaker leadership, in the wake of these very public cases, commenced using official indentures as a means of securing children; beginning in the early 1820s, proper legal documents were signed and witnessed when children were brought into the Society.

3. *Journal of the South Family, "Commencing with the adoption of the Am'ed Covenant--6th June 1830,"* original located at Western Reserve Historical Society [WRHS]; transcribed by Betty Shaver from microfilm in New York State Library , VB305. Transcribed records located at the Shaker Heritage Society, Albany, N.Y.

4. "Morrell Baker's Account of Shakers when He Came in 1791." Original at Western Reserve Historical Society *"Testimonies and Biographies, 1816-1912.* Reel 49 Also on microfilm at the New York State Library. "In the 7 years [since I] came they put up 12 buildings--a meeting house, a 'long shop' (2 stories, 3 rooms each floor) for the shoe-maker's shop, whip-maker, wheelwright, tailor, saddler & harness maker and where Father Hocknell lived ; [in addition a] spin shop, joiners shop, wash house, old office, tan house, south barn, saw mill. The log meeting house stood about 6 feet back of the front door of our present dwelling house. It was one story high, above the meeting room and in the west part... Father Hock-nell... used to walk the floor for hours at a time and sing. The boys had a room immediately under and could hear him sing and walk the floor."

5. *Daily Journal of the Second or West Family* at Watervliet, author is Seth Wells, original located at Western Reserve Historical Society [WRHS]; transcribed by Betty Shaver from microfilm in New York State Library, VB300, reel 46. Transcribed records located at the Shaker Heritage Society, Albany, N.Y.

6. *"Women's Testimonies in Defense of Mother Ann Lee (1827)"* quoted in Humez, pp. 45-46.

7. *"A Summary View of the Millennial Church, or United Society of Believers, commonly called Shakers..." Second edition, revised and improved. Republished by the United Society, with Approbation of the Ministry. Albany: 1848. Printed by C. Van Benthuysen.* Section 9-10, p. 4. New-York Historical Society Main Collection, BX9771 .A3

8. Extracted from a typewritten (copied) book containing a list of Shaker members who served in the Revolutionary War, this list is of the inform and needy dependents the Watervliet Society was caring for in January 1825. New York State Library Manuscripts and Special Collections, Shaker Collection, SC20330, Box 34, folders 16.

9. *"Memorandum of events of the Second Order, 1818-1836.* Feb 5, 1825. New York State Library Manuscripts and Special Collections, Shaker Collection, SC20330, Box 2, folder 1.

CHAPTER TWO

The Wicks Settle In

1. *"To the Elders, Deacons, Brethren & Sisters of the Society in Watervliet,"* an address by Seth Y. Wells, January 26, 1832. New York State Library Manuscripts an Special Collections, Shaker Collection, SC20330, Box 1, folder 20.

2. Wergland, Glendyne R. *Sisters in the Faith: Shaker Women and Equality of the Sexes.* Amherst, MA: University of Massachusetts Press, 2011. pp. 76-77.

3. *"Record of the South Family of the United Society, called Shakers, in the town of Watervliet, Albany County and State of New York... "* New York State Library Manuscripts and Special Collections, Shaker Collection, SC20330, Box 2, folder 3.

4. *"Memorandum of events of the Second Order, 1818-1836.* Feb 5, 1825. New York State Library Manuscripts and Special Collections, Shaker Collection, SC20330, Box 2, folder 1.

5. Ibid, various dates.

6. *"Record of the South Family of the United Society, called Shakers, in the town of Watervliet, Albany County and State of New York... "* New York State Library Manuscripts and Special Collections, Shaker Collection, SC20330, Box 2, folder 3.

CHAPTER THREE

Part One, The White Plague

1. Elizabeth Youngs, in a letter from Watervliet to her good friend Molly Goodrich, Jan. 26, 1829; Humez, Mother's First Born, p. 196

2. Miller and Fuller, Introduction, pp. 3 Miller, Amy Bess and Persis W.

Fuller. *The Best of Shaker Cooking.* New York, NY: Macmillan, 1985.

3. Ibid, p. xxv and p. 3

4. ibid p. 4.

5. *"The Ministerial Journal, 1834-1836,"* kept by Asenath Clark. Stephen Paterwic transcribed this journal and distributed copies to various sites including the Shaker Heritage Society.

6. "The consumpthing I expect" North Family journal

7. I.N.Y. April 21, 1838

8. *"Watervliet Prescriptions,"* New York State Library Manuscripts and Special Collections, Shaker Collection, SC20330, Box 40, folder 10.

9. Buckingham, Phoebe Ann. Oct. 4, 1842. *Diaries...* 26 bound volumes describing daily life at the Church Family in Watervliet, dating from 1837-1878. New York State Library, Manuscripts and Special Collections, Shaker Collection, SC20330, Boxes 5-9.

10. Isaac N. Youngs, various dates, 1843

11. Ibid, I.N.Y.

12. Murray, John E. *"The White Plague in Utopia: Tuberculosis in Nineteenth-Century Communes,"* Bulletin of the History of Medicine, 1994, 68: 278-306 (p. 288)

13. Ibid Murray, see table on p.289.

14. Ibid, Murray, p. 297.

15. Herbrandson, Dee. *Shaker Herbs and Their Medicinal Uses.* Albany, NY: Shaker Heritage Society, 1985.

16. Daily Journal of the Second or West Family at Watervliet, author is Seth Wells, original located at Western Reserve Historical Society [WRHS]; transcribed by Betty Shaver from microfilm in New York State Library , VB300, reel 46. Transcribed records located at the Shaker Heritage Society, Albany, N.Y. The Wicks girls' deaths were recorded in several places.

17. Medlicott, Carol. *Partake a Little Morsel: Popular Shaker Hymns of the Nineteenth Century.* Richard Couper Press, 2011. Hymn #24, p. 56.

CHAPTER THREE
Herbals Part 2

1. The herb picking and processing are mentioned variously in the Church Family diaries kept by *Phoebe Ann Buckingham* and her brother *David Austin Buckingham.* see individual dates. (Buckingham, Phoebe Ann. *Diaries...* 26 bound volumes describing daily life at the Church Family in Watervliet, dating from 1837-1878. New York State Library, Manuscripts and Special Collections, Shaker Collection, SC20330, Boxes 5-9. **AND** *"Records of the Church at Watervliet, NY."* by D.A. (David Austin) Buckingham. WHRS. Vol. 279.Transcribed by Betty Shaver from microfilm in New York State Library. VB321 Reel 47.Transcribed records located at the Shaker Heritage Society.

2. Herbrandson, p. 8, 10.

3. I.N.Y. December 1836

4. I.N.Y. October 1842 and summer 1843

5. I.N.Y. January 1844

CHAPTER FOUR
Era of Manifestations

1. Mary Wicks, instrument: WRHS-Inspired Writings, 1838-1842 *"A True Record of Sacred Communications; written by Divine Hand by the Mortal Hand of Chosen Instruments; at the Church at New Lebanon"* microfilm at Hamilton College Chapter XVII pp. 174-175.

2. I.N.Y. Dec. 8, 1836

3. I.N.Y. Summary for the end of the year, 1836.

4. "bury the earthly home of Ann ..." August 28, 1832. *Daily Journal of the Second or West Family* at Watervliet, author is Seth Wells, original located at Western Reserve Historical Society [WRHS]; transcribed by Betty Shaver from microfilm in New York State Library , A FM-22, VB300, reel 46. Transcribed records located at the Shaker Heritage Society, Albany, N.Y.

5. "100 sleighs and cutters" Rufus Bishop Jan 31, 1831

6. *"Record of the South Family of the United Society, called Shakers, in the town of Watervliet, Albany County and State of New York...* " New York State Library Manuscripts and Special Collections, Shaker Collection, SC20330, Box 2, folder 3.

7. I.N.Y. January 1837

8. Rufus Bishop, January 1837

9. Rufus Bishop, Jan. 1837

10. On the 27th of January, 1855, David Austin Buckingham notes in his journal *The Records of the Church at Watervliet:* "Oliver Prentiss of the 2nd family settled off with the Believers last Thursday and has gone to the world to enjoy what he can of the world, flesh and devil." Poor Oliver Prentiss wrestled often with his conscience, but seems to have lost the battle. He moves to Hoosick at this time. And see chapter 6, "The Wicks in the World." Eventually Oliver Prentiss actually moved back into the Shaker world, regaining his privilege at New Lebanon. Note: the original *"Records of the Church at Watervliet"* are located at Western Reserve Historical Society [WRHS]; transcribed by Betty Shaver from microfilm in New York State Library , VB281. Transcribed records located at the Shaker Heritage Society, Albany, N.Y.

11. *"Record of the South Family of the United Society, called Shakers, in the town of Watervliet, Albany County and State of New York...* " New York State Library Manuscripts and Special Collections, Shaker Collection, SC20330, Box 2, folder 3.

12. Rufus Bishop, September 1837

13. Rufus Bishop Sabbath Day, December 31, 1837

14. I.N.Y. Saturday May 19, 1838

15. Rufus Bishop, November and December 1838.

16. "Happified spirits" *"Journal of Inspired Meetings, 1841."* 1 v. 200 p. New York State Library Manuscripts and Special Collections, Shaker Collection, SC20330, Box 2, folder 2.

17. Rufus Bishop May 23, 1835

18. Rufus Bishop May 16, 17, 1839

19. Rufus Bishop 1839, Feb. 27

20. Mary Wicks, instrument: WRHS-Inspired Writings, 1838-1842 "A True Record of Sacred Communications; written by Divine Hand by the Mortal Hand of Chosen Instruments; at the Church at New Lebanon" Chapter XVII microfilm at Hamilton College. pp. 174-175 21. CLARIFY

21. *"butternut tree"* 28 April, 1842 *"Daily Journal of the First Order or the Church Family"* (at this point probably kept by David Austin Buckingham); original is located at WRHS (Western Reserve Historical Society); Betty Shaver transcribed from microfilm, Reel 47, VB 321. Her transcriptions are located at the Shaker Heritage Society.

22. Rufus Bishop July 28, 1844.

23. Rufus Bishop July 28, 1844.

24. *Records of the Church Meeting Journal at Watervliet,* NY. 1844-1846, original in Library of Congress, BX9768 W2W Betty Shaver transcribed from microfilm, A-FM 22, Roll 9. Her transcriptions are located at the Shaker Heritage Society.

25. Rufus Bishop, June 4, 1843.

26. Foster, Salem versus Watervliet visions, p.56

27. Rufus Bishop Sept. 7, 1843

28. Humez, p. 22

CHAPTER FIVE
Earthly Love

Mary and Derobigne

1. *"Record of the South Family of the United Society, called Shakers, in the town of Watervliet, Albany County and State of New York..."*] New York State Library Manuscripts and Special Collections, Shaker Collection, SC20330, Box 2, folder 3.

2. *"Millennial Laws, or, Gospel Statutes and Ordinances Adapted to the day of Christ's Second Appearing..."* Recorded at New Lebanon, August 7th, 1821. Revived & re-established by the Ministry and Elders, October 1845. 2 v. 142-214 p. New York State Library Manuscripts and Special Collections, Shaker Collection, SC20330, Box 17, folders 1-2

3. Bennett, Derobigne Mortimer. *The World's Sages, Thinkers and Reformers, being Biographical Sketches of Leading Philosophers, Teachers, Skeptics, Innovators, Founders of New Schools of Thought, etc.* New York: D.M. Bennett, 1878. [Public domain] p. 1061

4. Ibid p. 1061

5. Ibid p.1061

6. Ibid p.1061

7. I.N.Y. Jan. 1, 1840

8. I.N.Y. October 1843

9. I.N.Y. October 1843

10. I.N.Y. 9/28/1843

11. P.A.B. Various dates, summer and early fall, 1838.

12. I.N.Y. Various dates, July 1843

13. I.N.Y. April 14, 1843

14. After the "Great Disappointment," a number of the disillusioned turned to the Shakers for comfort-- Shaker theology also hailed Christ's Second Appearance--and various downcast "Millerites" sought spiritual and physical refuge at New Lebanon and Watervliet. A core group of "ex-Millerites" went on to form what became what is today known as the Seventh Day Adventist Church.

15. (Theodore Noyes' visit to the Shakers). Wonderley, Anthony. "Watervliet Shakers through the Eyes of the Oneida Perfectionists, 1863-1875. *"American Communal Societies Quarterly* April 2009, Vol. 3, No. 2. p. 52

16. "Brethren reading" Rufus Bishop July 1844

17. Bennett, " *The World's Sages...* p. 1063

18. I.N.Y. 9/12/1846

19. R.B. 9/12/1846

20. R.B. 9/12/1846

21. I.N.Y. 9/12/1846

22. Bennett, " *The World's Sages...* p. 1063

23. Ibid, p. 1064

24. I.N.Y. Sept. 14, 1846 and Sept. 18, 1846.

Loren and Arabella

1. *Phoebe Ann Buckingham.* Box 5, Vol. 1 Jan. 1, 1835

2. Ibid Box 5, Vol. 2 March 1837

3. Ibid. Box 5, Vol. 2 July 1838

4. *Rufus Bishop,* April 1839

5. *"Records of the Church at Watervliet, NY.* by D.A. (David Austin) Buckingham. WHRS. Vol. 279. Transcribed by Betty Shaver from microfilm in New York State Library. VB321 Reel 47. Transcribed records located at the Shaker Heritage Society. Date: October 12, 1843

6. *Phoebe Ann Buckingham.* Box 5, Vol. 2 Various dates

7. *Rufus Bishop* and *South Family Journal*; various entries during January 1832.

8. *Isaac Newton Youngs,* April 1837 The Shakers were constantly trying to get their young men excused from military service.

9. *"Records of the Church at Watervliet, NY.* by D.A. (David Austin) Buckingham. WHRS. Vol. 279. Transcribed by Betty Shaver from microfilm in New York State Library. VB321 Reel 47. Transcribed records located at the Shaker Heritage Society. Date: September 2, 1842

10. *Rufus Bishop,* June 27, 1844 and July 1, 1844.

11. *Phoebe Ann Buckingham* Box 5, vol. 3 Aug. 17, 1848

12. *Phoebe Ann Buckingham* Box 5, vol. 5 Nov. 7, 1850

13. *Phoebe Ann Buckingham* Nov. 29 and Dec 2, 1852 Box 5 Vol.3

14. July, South Family Journal, VB-306, or original [Betty Shaver, VB 306 p.14--check this].

15. "Indentures of children adopted by Watervliet Shaker families, 1832-1872. New York State Library Manuscripts and Special Collections, Shaker Collection, SC20330, Box 41

16. *Phoebe Ann Buckingham* January 1853

CHAPTER SIX

The Wicks in the World

The LOST BOYS, Thomas, William, Braman

Pt. 1 Thomas

1. Western Reserve Historical Society, Shaker Manuscripts, Shaker Membership Card File: Reel 123 (microfilm exists at multiple locations)

2. Massachusetts Vital Records Project: *The Vital Records of Ashfield, MA to the end of the year 1849."*

Pt. 2 William

1. Western Reserve Historical Society, Shaker Manuscripts, Shaker Membership Card File: Reel 123 (microfilm exists at multiple locations)

2. *U.S. Army Register of Enlistments,* 1798-1914, Ancestry. com "Provided in Association with the National Archives and Records Administration."

3. Ibid.

4. Ibid.

5. Ibid.

Pt. 3 Braman

1. I.N.Y. October 20, 1842.

2. Andrews, Edward D. *The Community Industries of the Shakers.* Facsimile Reprint of New York State Museum Handbook Number 15. [1933] University of the State of New York, Emporium Publications: 1971. p. 229

3. I.N.Y. Nov. 17, 1842 and Feb.4 1843

4. I.N.Y. Sept. 2nd and 3rd 1843

5. R.B. Aug. 24, 1847.

6. *"Louisville Morning Courier,"* courtesy of the Kentucky Historical Society

7. R.B. Sept. 4, 1848

The "Truth Seekers"

1. Bennett, Derobigne Mortimer. *The World's Sages, Thinkers and Reformers, being Biographical Sketches of Leading Philosophers, Teachers, Skeptics, Innovators, Founders of New Schools of Thought, etc.* New York: D.M. Bennett, 1878. p. 1064

2. Bradford, Roderick *D.M. Bennett: The Truth Seeker* Amherst, New York: Prometheus Books: 2006. p.54

3. Bennett p. 1065-1066

4. Bradford, p. 68, (quoting from *The Truth Seeker: A Journal of Freethought and Reform"* Nov 25, 1882).

5. Bennett, p. 1071

6. Grateful thanks to Roderick Bradford for sharing this interesting fact.

7. See Roderick Bradford , *D.M. Bennett: The Truth Seeker chapter 18, "Behind Bars."*

8. Evans, Frederick William. Autobiography of a Shaker: And Revelation of the Apocalypse, With An Appendix. New York: American News Company, 1888. p.6

9. Ibid, p. 8

10. Ibid p. 9

11. Bradford, Roderick. *D.M. Bennett: The Truth Seeker.* Amherst, New York: Prometheus Books: 2006. p. 119-120 (footnoted/reprinted from *The Truth Seeker: A Journal of Freethought and Reform"* Jan. 19, 1878).

Part 3. Angeline

1. I.N.Y. August 1843

2. *Daily Journal of the Second or West Family at Watervliet*, author is Seth Wells, original located at Western Reserve Historical Society [WRHS]; transcribed by Betty Shaver from microfilm in New York State Library , VB300, reel 46. Transcribed records located at the Shaker Heritage Society, Albany, N.Y. The Wicks girls' deaths were recorded in several journals.

3. Daily Journal of the Second or West Family at Watervliet, author is Seth Wells, original located at Western Reserve Historical Society[WRHS]; transcribed by Betty Shaver from microfilm in New York State Library , VB300, reel 46. Transcribed records located at the Shaker Heritage Society, Albany, N.Y. The Wicks girls' deaths were recorded in several places.

4. NY State 1855 Census records, which by this time had become much more detailed, including data about the value of real estate, etc.

5. I.N.Y. March 29, 1838

6. P.A.B. January 25, 1855

7. NY State 1855 Census records

8. R.B. Nov. 20th, 22nd 1834 and Feb. 12th, 13th, 17th 1835

9. Calarco, Tom. *The Underground Railroad in the Adirondack Region.* Jefferson, NC: McFarland, 2004. pp. 95, 197.

10. New York, Wills and Probate Records, 1659-1999 for Garret Van Hoosen, April 7, 1857.

11. "Presbyterian Church Baptismal and Membership Records, 1815-1871," *townofschaghticoke.org.* (courtesy of Chris Kelly, Schaghticoke (NY) Town Historian).

12. New York, Wills and Probate Records, 1659-1999 for Parmelia Wicks

13. New York State Archives/ *New York, State Census, 1870* [online: Provo, UT: Ancestry.com Provided in association with National Archives and Records Administration]

14. New York, Wills and Probate Records, 1659-1999, for John M. Percey

15. *1900 Federal Census for California, Los Angeles, Pasadena Precinct 05, District 0117.* [online: Provo, UT: Ancestry.com Provided in association with National Archives and Records Administration]

Part 4. Loren the Linchpin

1. Bennett, Derobigne Mortimer. *The World's Sages, Thinkers and Reformers, being Biographical Sketches of Leading Philosophers, Teachers, Skeptics, Innovators, Founders of New Schools of Thought, etc.* New York: D.M. Bennett, 1878. p. 1064

2. Brewer, Priscilla J. *Shaker Communities, Shaker Lives,* Hanover, NH: University Press of New England, 1988. p. 153.

3. I.N.Y. October 1843

4. United States Patent and Trademark Office: All of Loren's patents were filed with the *United States Patent Office,* their numbers and complete descriptions are available on line. http://www.uspto.gov/web/

5. *New York Daily Tribune, 9/8/1860.* Proquest Historical Newspapers: New York Tribune, Herald Tribune, p.10

6. " Now my dear Companions." *"Song Sheets"* compiled by Dale Spencer for the *Shaker Seminar 2014,* held in Sabbathday Lake, presented by Hancock Shaker Village.

7. Email correspondence with Jhon Usmanov, staffer at the Green-Wood Cemetery, March 21, 2016.

8. Bradford, Roderick. *D.M. Bennett: The Truth Seeker.* Amherst, New York: Prometheus Books: 2006. p. 376-377.

9. Ibid, Bradford, p. 378

10. " O Ho the Pretty Chain" "Song Sheets" compiled by Dale Spencer

for the *Shaker Seminar 2014*, held in Sabbathday Lake, presented by Hancock Shaker Village.

CHAPTER SEVEN

The Last Shakers

1. *"Record of the South Family of the United Society, called Shakers, in the town of Watervliet, Albany County and State of New York..."* New York State Library Manuscripts and Special Collections, Shaker Collection, SC20330, Box 2, folder 3. Article V, Section 2

2. *"Record of the South Family of the United Society, called Shakers, in the town of Watervliet, Albany County and State of New York..."* New York State Library Manuscripts and Special Collections, Shaker Collection, SC20330, Box 2, folder 3

3. Ibid.

4. RB 6/15/1848

5. *"Record of the South Family of the United Society, called Shakers, in the town of Watervliet, Albany County and State of New York..."* New York State Library Manuscripts and Special Collections, Shaker Collection, SC20330, Box 2, folder 3

6. Ibid.

7. Avery, Giles B. *"A Register of Incidents and Events...kept by Giles Avery."* 1859 Oct. 2- 1874- Dec. 21. 1 vol. (645 p.) New York Public Library, Humanities and Social Sciences Division, Manuscripts and Archives Division, Shaker Manuscript Collection, 1780- 1952. Wed. June 3, 1863.

AFTERWARD

1. "A Visit to Our Old Home." *The Truth Seeker: A Journal of Freethought and Reform,"* D.M. Bennett. July 31, 1880 Taken from a bibliography compiled by David Newell and Cass Nawrocki in the *American Communal Societies Quarterly,* Vol. 9, nos. 3 & 4, pp. 132. (and thank you to Rod Bradford for the *"Truth Seeker"* article in full)

2. Paterwic, Stephen J. *Historical Dictionary of the Shakers.* Historical Dictionaries of Religions, Philosophies, and Movements, No. 87; Latham, MD: Scarecrow, 2008. p. 71

3. Ibid, p. 71

4. Brown, David. "Shakerism" from *"Human Nature: A Monthly Journal of Holistic Science, 1876.* Taken from a bibliography compiled by David Newell and Cass Nawrocki in the *American Communal Societies Quarterly,* Vol. 9, nos. 3 & 4 [July and October 2015] pp. 132.

5. Bradford, Roderick. *D.M. Bennett: The Truth Seeker.* Amherst, New York: Prometheus Books: 2006. p. 378.

6. *"Millennial Laws, or, Gospel Statutes and Ordinances Adapted to the day of Christ's Second Appearing..."* Recorded at New Lebanon, August 7th, 1821. Revived & re-established by the Ministry and Elders, October 1845. 2 v. 142-214 p. New York State Library Manuscripts and Special Collections, Shaker Collection, SC20330, Box 17, folders 1-2

7. Address: *"Circular Epistle to our precious Brethren and Sisters in Zion [at Watervliet]. By the ministry at Mt. Lebanon, June 23, 1870.* 20 p. NYSL Box 16, folder 3.

BIBLIOGRAPHY

American Communal Societies Quarterly : a publication of Hamilton College, Richard Couper Press. Editor: Randall L. Ericson. Various issues.

Andrews, Edward D. *The Community Industries of the Shakers.* Facsimile Reprint of New York State Museum Handbook Number 15. [1933] University of the State of New York, Emporium Publications: 1971

Andrews, Edward D. *The People Called Shakers: A Search for a Perfect Society.* New York: Dover Publications, 1963.

Andrews, Edward Deming, and Faith Andrews. *Shaker Furniture: the Craftsmanship of an American Communal Sect.* New York, NY: Dover Publications, 1933.

Avery, Giles B. *"A Register of Incidents and Events...kept by Giles Avery."* 1859 Oct. 2 [through] 1874 Dec. 21. 1 vol. (645 p.) New York Public Library, Humanities and Social Sciences Division, Manuscripts and Archives Division, Shaker Manuscript Collection, 1780-1952.

Barkun, Michael. *Crucible of the Millennium: the Burned-Over District of New York in the 1840s.* Syracuse, New York: Syracuse University Press, 1986.

Bates, Issachar. *A Sketch of the Life and Experiences of Issacker[sic]* Bates, 1836. 1 v. 149 (240) p. New York State Library Manuscripts and Special Collections, Shaker Collection, SC20330, Box 20, folder 1. Note: this is a copy of the original, the Shakers produced a number of handwritten copies of the Bates autobiography; the original seems to have been lost.

Bennett, Derobigne Mortimer. T*he World's Sages, Thinkers and Reformers, being Biographical Sketches of Leading Philosophers, Teachers, Skeptics, Innovators, Founders of New Schools of Thought, etc.* New York: D.M. Bennett, 1878. [Public domain]

Binney, Charles James Fox. *The History and Genealogy of the Prentice, Or Prentiss Family, in New England, etc. From 1631 to 1863.* Boston, 1883. [Public domain]

Bishop, Rufus. *A Journal of Passing Events: begun January 1st, 1830. By Rufus Bishop, in the 56th year of his age. Journal 1830-1839 May 18.* [and ensuing volumes] New York Public Library, Humanities and Social Sciences Division, Manuscripts and Archives Division, Shaker Manuscript Collection, 1780-1952.

Bishop, Rufus, and Seth Youngs Wells. *Testimonies of the life, character, revelations and doctrines of Mother Ann Lee, and the elders with her: through whom the Word of Eternal Life was opened this days, of Christ's second appearing...* Albany, NY: 1888. [Public domain]

Blinn, Henry C. *The Manifestation of Spiritualism Among the Shakers.* East Canterbury, NH: The Shakers, 1899. [Public domain]

Boice, Martha, et al. *Maps of the Shaker West: A Journey of Discovery.* Dayton, Oh: Knot Garden Press, 1997.

Bradford, Roderick. *D.M. Bennett: The Truth Seeker.* Amherst, New York: Prometheus Books: 2006.

Brewer, Priscilla J. *Shaker Communities, Shaker Lives,* Hanover, NH: University Press of New England, 1988.

Brown, Thomas. *An Account of the People called Shakers: their Faith, Doctrines, and Practices Exemplified in the Life, Conversations and Experience of the Author During the Time He Belonged to the Society: To Whoich is Affixed A History of their Rise and Progress To the Present Day. by Thomas Brown Troy N.Y. : Printed by Parker and Bliss : Sold at the Troy Bookstore; by Websters and Skinners, ; and by S. Wood, New-York;1812.* New-York Historical Society Main Collection Y1812.

Buckingham, Phoebe Ann. *Diaries...* 26 bound volumes describing daily life at the Church Family in Watervliet, dating from 1837-1878. New York State Library, Manuscripts and Special Collections, Shaker Collection, SC20330, Boxes 5-9. [Note: earlier volumes may actually have been kept by Lydia Annas]

Bushman, Richard Lyman. *Joseph Smith: Rough Stone Rolling.* New York: Alfred A. Knopf, 2005.

Calarco, Tom. *The Underground Railroad in the Adirondack Region.* Jefferson, NC: McFarland, 2004.

Campion, Nardi Reeder. *Mother Ann Lee: Morning Star of the Shakers.* Hanover, NH: University Press of New England, 1990.

Carr, Sister Frances A. *Growing Up Shaker.* New Gloucester, Maine: The United Society of Shakers, 1995.

Carr, Sister Frances A. *Shaker Your Plate: Of Shaker Cooks and Cooking.* New Gloucester, Maine, The Shaker Society (Distributed by the University Press of New England): 1985.

Catalogue of Medicinal Plants and Vegetable Medicines. Prepared in the United Society, Watervliet, N.Y. Hudson N.Y. : Printed by Ashbel Stoddard, 1833, Cover title. 8 p.New York State Library, Manuscripts and Special Collections, Shaker Collection, SC20330, Box 42, folder 43.

Chapman, Eunice. *"An Account of the People called Shakers: in the case of Eunice Chapman and her children, since her husband became acquainted with those people, written by herself..."* Albany: printed by the authoress, at number 95 State-street, five doors east of the Episcopal church, 1817. New-York Historical Society Main Collection.Y1817 .C

"Circular Epistle to our precious Brethren and Sisters in Zion..." [at Watervliet]. By the ministry at Mt. Lebanon, June 23, 1870. 20 p. New York State Library Manuscripts and Special Collections, Shaker Collection, SC20330, Box 16, folder 3.

Daily Journal of the Second or West Family at Watervliet, author is Seth Wells, original located at Western Reserve Historical Society [WRHS]; transcribed by Betty Shaver from microfilm in New York State Library , VB300, reel 46. Transcribed records located at the Shaker Heritage Society, Albany, N.Y.

Dyer, Mary. *A Brief Statement of the Sufferings of Mary Dyer: Occasioned by the Society Called Shakers. Written by Herself...*Boston: William Spear, 1818. [Public Domain: New York Public Library]

Evans, Frederick William. *Autobiography of a Shaker: And Revelation of the Apocalypse, With An Appendix.* New York: American News Company, 1888.

Foster, Lawrence. *Women, Family, and Utopia: Communal Experiments of the Shakers, the Oneida Community, and the Mormons.* Syracuse, NY: Syracuse University Press, 1991.

The Gift of Inspiration: Art of the Shakers, 1830-1888, May 3-May 29, 1979. [Exhibit Catalog] Hirschl & Adler Galleries, New York, New York.

Godwin, Joscelyn. *Upstate Cauldron: Eccentric Spiritual Movements in Early New York State.* Albany, NY: State University of New York Press, 2015.

Herbrandson, Dee *Shaker Herbs and Their Medicinal Uses.* Albany, NY: Shaker Heritage Society, 1985.

Hinds, William Alfred. *American Communities* New York, NY: Corinth Books [American Experience series, reprint from 1878], 1961.

Hulings, Martha A. *Shaker Days Remembered.* Albany, NY: Shaker Heritage Society, 1983.

Humez, Jean M. [editor]. *Mother's First-Born Daughters: Early Shaker Writings on Women and Religion.* Bloomington, IN: Indian University Press, 1993.

Jennings, Chris. *Paradise Now: The Story of American Utopianism.* New York: Random House, 2016.

"Journal of Inspired Meetings, 1841." 1 v. 200 p. New York State Library Manuscripts and Special Collections, Shaker Collection, SC20330, Box 2, folder 2.

Journal of the South Family, "Commencing with the adoption of the Am'ed Covenant--6th June 1830" VB. 305, original located at Western Reserve Historical Society [WRHS]; transcribed by Betty Shaver from microfilm in New York State Library , VB305. Transcribed records located at the Shaker Heritage Society, Albany, N.Y.

Kirk, John T. *The Shaker World: Art, Life, Belief.* New York, NY: Harry N. Abrams, 1997.

Meacham, Joseph. *"A Concise Statement of the Principles of the Only True Church of Christ, by Joseph Meacham Together with a Letter from James Whittaker to his Natural Relations in England, Printed at Bennington Vermon by Haskell & Russell, 1790."* [Reprinted in the United Society, Canterbury, N.H. 1847]

Medlicott, Carol. "Conflict and Tribulation on the Frontier: the West Union Shakers and Their Retreat." *American Communal Societies Quarterly,* Vol. 3, No. 3 (July 2009): 111-137

Medlicott, Carol. *Partake a Little Morsel: Popular Shaker Hymns of the Nineteenth Century.* Hamilton, NY: Richard Couper Press: 2011.

Medlicott, Carol. *Issachar Bates: A Shaker's Journey.* Hanover, NH: University Press of New England, 2013.

Melcher, Marguerite Fellows. *The Shaker Adventure.* Old Chatham, NY: The Shaker Museum, 1986.

"A Memorandum Book Beginning in the year 1818..." [anonymous journal] New York State Library Manuscripts and Special Collections, Shaker Collection, SC20330, Box 2, folder 1.

"Millennial Laws, or, Gospel Statutes and Ordinances Adapted to the day of Christ's Second Appearing..." Recorded at New Lebanon, August 7th, 1821. Revived & re-established by the Ministry and Elders, October 1845. 2 v. 142-214 p. New York State Library Manuscripts and Special Collections, Shaker Collection, SC20330, Box 17, folders 1-2

Miller, Amy Bess and Persis W. Fuller. *The Best of Shaker Cooking.* New York, NY: Macmillan, 1985.

"Morrell Baker's Account of Shakers when He Came in 1791. Original at Western Reserve Historical Society *"Testimonies and Biographies, 1816-1912."* Reel 49.

Morse, Flo. *The Shakers and the World's People.* Hanover, NH: University Press of New England, 1987.

Morse, Flo. *The Story of the Shakers.* Woodstock, VT: Countryman Press, 1986.

Murray, John E. "The White Plague in Utopia: Tuberculosis in Nineteenth-Century Communes," *Bulletin of the History of Medicine,* 1994, 68: 278-306 (p. 288)

Nordhoff, Charles. *The Communistic Societies of the United States, From Personal Visit and Observation.* New York, NY: Dover, 1966.

Paterwic, Stephen J. *Historical Dictionary of the Shakers.* Historical Dictionaries of Religions, Philosophies, and Movements, No. 87; Latham, MD: Scarecrow Press, 2008.

Patterson, Daniel W. *Gift Drawing and Gift Song: A Study of Two Forms of Shaker Inspiration.* Sabbathday Lake, Maine: The United Society of Shakers, 1983.

"Record of the South Family of the United Society, called Shakers, in the town of Watervliet, Albany County and State of New York..." New York State Library Manuscripts and Special Collections, Shaker Collection, SC20330, Box 2, folder 3.

"Rules and orders for Church of Christ's second appearing, established by the ministers and elders of the church;" revised and established by the same, Mount Lebanon, N.Y. May 1860. 3 v. 83-112p. New York State Library Manuscripts and Special Collections, Shaker Collection, SC20330, Box 18, folders 1-3.

Sanchez, Anita. *Mr. Lincoln's Chair: the Shakers and Their Quest for Peace.* McDonald & Woodward Publishing, 2009.

Sears, Hal D. *The Sex Radicals: Free Love in High Victorian America.* Lawrence, KS: Regents Press, 1977.

"Song Sheets" compiled by Dale Spencer for the Shaker Seminar 2014, held in Sabbathday Lake, presented by Hancock Shaker Village.

Stein, Stephen J. *The Shaker Experience in America: A History of the United Society of Believers.* New Haven, CT: Yale University Press, 1992.

"A Summary View of the Millennial Church, or United Society of Believers, commonly called Shakers..." Second edition, revised and improved. Republished by the United Society, with Approbation of the Ministry. Albany: 1848. Printed by C. Van Benthuysen. Section 9-10, p. 4. New York Historical Society Main Collection. BX9781 .A3

Testimonies of the Life, Character, Revelations and Doctrines of Mother Ann Lee and the Elders with her...in this day of Christ's Second Appearing, Collected from Living Witnesses, in Union with the Church..." Albany, NY: Weed, Parsons & Co., 1888.

"A Visit to our old home," Bennett, Derobigne Mortimer. *The Truth Seeker: A Journal of Freethought and Reform."* July 31, 1880

Wells, Seth Y. *"An Address on the education of children,"* January 26, 1832. 3 (4) p. New York State Library Manuscripts and Special Collections, Shaker Collection, SC20330, Box 1, folder 20.

Wergland, Glendyne R. *Sisters in the Faith: Shaker Women and Equality of the Sexes.* Amherst, MA: University of Massachusetts Press, 2011.

Woo, Ilyon. *The Great Divorce: A Nineteenth Century Mother's Extraordinary Fight Against Her Husband, the Shakers, and Her Times.* New York: NY: Atlantic Monthly Press, 2010.

Youngs, Isaac N. A *Domestic journal of daily occurrences kept by Isaac N. Youngs, January 1, 1834- December 31, 1846.* 1 vol. ca. 400 p. New York State Library Manuscripts and Special Collections, Shaker Collection, SV20330, Box 19, folder 1.

INDEX